PRAYING THROUGH IT

Pursuing a Heart of Prayer

LORI BOYD

KAIO PUBLICATIONS, INC.

ISBN-13: 978-1-952955-04-4

Published by Kaio Publications
http://www.kaiopublications.org

Printed in the United States of America

Cover Design: Ben Giselbach

To Sam,
the answer to my prayers

Contents

PRAYING THROUGH IT

Acknowledgments

Thank you...

...to the encouragement givers, the prayer lifters, and the hope spreaders.

...to those who uphold light and love in times of peace as well as in times of pandemic.

...to the ones who choose faith and love over fear and hate.

...to the dreamers, the believers, and the doers of good.

...to all of you who endure trials with strength and grace while glorifying God—for teaching me that the best way to do it is to keep praying through it!

The Privilege of Prayer

AS we begin to talk about prayer, answering the question "Why?" seems like a good place to start. **Why** do we pray? **Why** should it be part of who we are and what we do? The answer very simply is this: **Prayer is the means by which we communicate with God.** It's how we talk to our Heavenly Father! It's the way that we are able to approach Him on His throne. The ability for you and me to be in the presence of God happens through Jesus Christ in the form of prayer. As Christians, this most extraordinary privilege should be woven in and around every part of every day. We follow the instruction to "pray without ceasing" found in 1 Thessalonians 5:17, because we want God to be present and involved in everything that we do. And that's really what prayer is doing—it's connecting us with God.

Prayer is vital to our spiritual health and spiritual growth. It helps keep us spiritually strong! Think about prayer as a power cord that connects us to our Power Source. We live in a very technical world and use electronic devices in almost everything that we do. We know how important it is that they stay charged! When you look at your phone and you see that you're getting down to 5 or 10 percent power, you know you need to grab a power cord and get charged up or that cell phone is going to die. That's the idea with prayer. You are the cell phone and you will start to lose power if you don't stay connected to God. Prayer is how we stay "plugged in" to our divine Power Source. If we try to continue running on low power, we are at risk for spiritual death. We have to be sure that we are staying charged by talking to God through prayer and then openly receiving His guidance and instruction through the reading and studying of His Word.

The number one reason for praying is that it allows us to have direct communication with our powerful Creator, but there's more! Let's consider eight more reasons **why** we should pray.

We pray because...

1. WE PRAY BECAUSE GOD IS OUR FATHER. Not only is God our Father, but He is also a good Father. Romans 8:16-17 says, "*The Spirit Himself bears witness with our spirit, that we are children of God. And if children, then heirs, heirs of God, and joint heirs with Christ if indeed we suffer with Him, that we may also be glorified together.*" We are **children** of God! First John 3:1 also says, "*Behold what manner of love the Father has bestowed on us, that we should be called children of God. Therefore the world does not know us because it did not know Him.*" As a good father loves his children, so God loves us and wants us to talk to Him. Imagine God looking down on His children and seeing that we're in distress, seeing that we're hurting, seeing that we're struggling, and wanting so desperately for us to come to Him. I can almost hear Him calling out, "Talk to Me! I'm the one who can help you!" The truth is, God knows exactly what's going on in our lives. We don't have to tell Him. He knows. But the beautiful truth is that He **wants** us to talk to Him. He wants us to turn those troubles and those difficulties over to Him. Remember that God is your Father, He is a good Father, and He wants to know what's happening in the lives of His children.

2. WE PRAY BECAUSE WE NEED GOD'S HELP. Hebrews 4:16 says, "*Let us therefore come boldly to the throne of grace, that we may obtain mercy and find grace to help in times of need.*" In some versions, the words mercy and grace have been translated "compassion" and "pardon," or "kindness" and "favor." Prayer is a reflection of our dependence on God. Our strength is limited, but God's strength is limitless. We need God's help and He stands ready to pour out His mercy and grace in our times of need. Listen to His words found in Isaiah 41:10, "*Fear not, for I am with you; be not dismayed, for I am your God. I will strengthen you, yes, I will help you, I will uphold you with My righteous right hand.*"

Prayer is a reflection of our dependence on God.

3. WE PRAY BECAUSE WE LOVE GOD. Prayer is not a burden. It is a blessing! It is a good thing! Talking to Him should be an absolute joy as we remember all the things that He has done for us and all that He has given to us. God is the giver of good gifts (James 1:17), the One who has bestowed all kinds of blessings on us, with the greatest of all being the gift of His Son Jesus Christ (John 3:16). Sin separated us from God, but through Jesus, He has provided us with a way back so that we are able to spend eternity at home with Him in Heaven. We love Him for the kindness and love He has so freely extended to us, and because we love Him, we should want to share our lives with Him. Relationships are never stagnant; they are constantly moving, either closer together or

further apart. When there is no communication between two people, their relationship will suffer. Talking to God will draw you closer to Him. It will strengthen and nurture your relationship. Prayer is a wonderful thing because it allows us a way to have meaningful conversations with the One we love the most.

4. **WE PRAY BECAUSE GOD ANSWERS PRAYERS.** Jesus spoke these words to His followers, "*So I say to you, 'Ask, and it will be given to you; seek, and you will find; knock, and it will be opened to you.' For everyone who asks receives; and he who seeks finds; and to him who knocks it will be opened*" (Luke 11:9-10). God welcomes our requests and has promised to grant them if we ask in faith and according to His will. Don't be like the people James describes in chapter four of his letter--the people who don't have because they don't ask! James also describes what **did** happen when the prophet Elijah asked God for something specific in prayer. James 5:17-18 says, "*Elijah was a man with a nature like ours; and he prayed earnestly that it would not rain, and it did not rain on the land for three years and six months. And he prayed again, and the heaven gave rain and the earth produced its fruit.*" This is a testimony to the fact that God hears and answers prayer. Elijah prayed earnestly, God heard him, and then God responded to his prayers. We may not always understand how or why God answers in a particular way, but we have confidence that He is listening and believe that He will do what is best for us. In Isaiah 55:8-9 we read, "'*For My thoughts are not your thoughts, nor are My ways your ways,' says the Lord; 'for as the heavens are higher than the earth, so are My ways higher than your ways, and My thoughts than your thoughts.*'" We don't have the mind of God, but we have faith that He is going to take care of our needs, sometimes in ways that we can't comprehend. We have to trust that under His providential care all things will work out for our good.

5. **WE PRAY BECAUSE IT IS A FORM OF SERVING AND OBEYING.** It is important for us to remember that prayer is not a suggestion. Prayer is an act of obedience. It is commanded throughout Scripture! Consider these verses:

> Matthew 5:44: "*Pray for those who persecute you.*"
>
> Romans 12:12: "*Be joyful in hope, patient in affliction, faithful in prayer.*"
>
> Ephesians 6:18: "*Praying always with all prayer and supplication in the Spirit, being watchful to this end with all perseverance and supplication for all the saints.*"
>
> Philippians 4:6: "*Do not be anxious about anything, but in everything by prayer and petition, with thanksgiving, present your requests to God.*"
>
> Colossians 4:2: "*Devote ourselves to prayer, being watchful and thankful.*"

1 Thessalonians 5:17: "*Pray without ceasing.*"

1 Timothy 2:1: "*I urge then first of all that requests, prayers, intercession and thanksgiving be made for everyone.*"

We pray because it is important and we want it to become a habit. We pray even if we don't understand it completely, even if we don't exactly know how it's working, or how God is hearing and answering. Although we may not fully grasp the ins and outs of prayer, we do it because God has commanded it. And when we pray, we're not just taking care of ourselves—we're serving others, too.

When you pray, you pray because you believe God is hearing you.

6. WE PRAY BECAUSE IT DEMONSTRATES OUR FAITH. We pray because we believe. We believe in our Creator and we confidently believe in His ability to answer our prayers. It's a testimony to others about our reliance on God. When somebody tells you something that is on his heart or something that she is struggling with and you say, "Would you mind if I pray with you about that?", you just gave them a brief glimpse into your own faith! What a wonderful example! When you pray, you pray because you believe that God is hearing you. You trust that He is listening and you believe that He **will** answer if it is consistent with His glory and His will. First John 5:14-15 reads, "*Now this is the confidence that we have in Him, that if we ask anything according to His will, He hears us. And if we know that He hears us, whatever we ask, we know that we have the petitions that we have asked of Him.*" That is a beautiful picture of faith in the action of prayer.

7. WE PRAY BECAUSE PRAYER IS A GIFT THAT COMES WITH BLESSING. Prayer strengthens us, relieves us, encourages us, and increases our faith; and as a result, our love for God will grow. Today, we can access God at any moment, but the ability to come before Him in prayer is not something we have always had as a blessing. In the Old Testament, not everybody could approach God—people could not directly come and bring their requests, and their praise, and their questions, and their concerns to God. It had to be done through somebody else. It had to be done through a priest or a prophet, or someone else chosen by God. But now, that is not the case! Now, everyone can approach the throne of God because Jesus is our intercessor. It is through Jesus that we can come to the Father and it is in His name that we pray. Prayer is truly a gift, and it results in a blessing of peace. Remember the words in Philippians 4:6-7, "*Be anxious for nothing, but in everything by prayer and supplication, with thanksgiving, let your requests be made known to God; and the peace of God, which surpasses all understanding, will guard your hearts and minds through Christ Jesus.*"

8. WE PRAY BECAUSE JESUS PRAYED. He is our perfect role model, and He prayed regularly. When Jesus was here on this earth, He knew the importance of staying in communication with His Father, and He did it all the time. There is example after example in Scripture of Jesus talking to His Father. Jesus often pulled away from the crowd and went to a quiet place where He could pray. Here are some references from the Bible that give a glimpse into the prayer life of Jesus:

Matthew 14:23: "*And when He had sent the multitudes away, He went up on the mountain by Himself to pray.*"

Matthew 26:36: "*Then Jesus came with them to a place called Gethsemane, and said to the disciples, 'Sit here while I go and pray over there.'*"

Mark 1:35: "*Now in the morning, having risen a long while before daylight, He went out and departed to a solitary place; and there He prayed.*"

Luke 5:16: "*So He Himself often withdrew into the wilderness and prayed.*"

Luke 6:12: "*Now it came to pass in those days that He went out to the mountain to pray, and continued all night in prayer to God.*"

I encourage you to look deeper into the stories around these verses and reflect on the flawless picture Jesus painted of the importance of prayer.

If we understand these reasons for prayer, what is it that keeps us from praying? What is it that gets in our way? We all have obstacles that we come in contact with throughout our days that hinder us, that keep us from this necessary aspect of our spiritual lives. We have to learn to recognize what those obstacles are and develop ways to either get rid of them completely or work around them so that we can be faithful in our prayer lives.

Prayer Obstacles

If I were to stop you right here and ask you to think, for just a second, about one thing that gets in your way of praying, what would come to your mind first? What is the biggest obstacle when it comes to your prayer life? What would your answer be? I have asked that question before when I have spoken on this subject, and the number one answer is typically the same. The greatest obstacle for most people is **time**. It's definitely mine. I feel like time often gets away from me. Sometimes as I work through all of the things that are on my to-do list for the day, prayer ends up taking a back seat, and before I know it, I'm getting into bed at night, hardly able to stay awake to talk to God. I try to start my day off with prayer and then talk to Him throughout the day, but if I'm not careful my day will become so filled with other things that I run out of time. Let's talk about three obstacles that get in the way of our prayer lives.

1. THE TIME OBSTACLE. What is really sad about this one (and this is painful for me because it's my greatest obstacle), is that when time is your obstacle to prayer, what you're really saying is, "I have more important things to do." That hits me right in my heart! In my mind, as I'm reviewing my list of what I have to accomplish that day, I'm thinking: "I have to do *this*, and I have to do *this*, and I have to do *this*, and *this*, and *this*, and *this*, and *that* is not as important." When we go through our day and we look at our schedules, we prioritize our tasks. We look at what we have to get done, and we complete the things that we feel we must get done. That's just what we do when we prioritize. And then we try to work prayer in, and it gets missed. We can't think so much about our own schedules, about all the things that we need to finish, all the things that we need to check off, and forget the importance of spending time with God and talking to Him.

You will never, ever, ever, ever regret time spent in prayer.

THE SOLUTION: We have to plan. We have to plan to be better at praying. We will never, ever, ever, ever regret time spent in prayer. There won't be time that we look back and say, "Oh, I spent wayyyy too much time in prayer that day." The truth is the more time that we spend in prayer, the more we get to know God and the better we communicate with Him. The more we communicate with God, the more comfortable it becomes. We're going to talk more about that when we get into some practical things to remember about prayer.

2. THE WORDS OBSTACLE. I think sometimes we might say, "I don't know what to say when it's time to pray. I don't even know how to **begin**. I can't think of the words. When I try to formulate words, it doesn't sound right or I sound silly. It's just hard for me." Listen. That is the flesh talking, **not** the spirit talking. Because the flesh would have us become spiritually lazy. The world says that nothing should be hard. If it's hard for you to do something, then don't bother doing it. It should come easy. And that's really just not true.

THE SOLUTION: We need to practice. The Bible tells us in Romans 8:26-27 that we have help from the Holy Spirit. Don't forget that! The Holy Spirit is helping us when the words aren't coming and we can't express what it is that we want to say. But, we have to practice. The *Merriam-Webster Dictionary* defines practice as "the activity of doing something again and again in order to become better at it" and "something that is done often or regularly." The more you pray, the easier it gets, and the more comfortable you will become doing it. Stay tuned! We're going to talk more about this when we get to the practical tips for praying.

3. **THE DOUBT OBSTACLE.** This is saying, "I don't know if I trust God's plan for my life. I don't know if He really hears. I don't seem to be getting an answer from Him, so I don't really know that prayer works." Those are some things you might think if doubt is an obstacle in your prayer life. This is a sign of faith that needs to be built up. Think about the Canaanite woman whose story we read in Matthew 15:21-28. She begged for mercy and did not receive the response she wanted. She worshiped and said, "Lord, help me!" and again she was told "no." She asked a third time and Jesus answered her prayer. She kept asking. Jesus had an important lesson to teach about faith, not only for the Canaanite woman, but also for everyone listening to Him that day and for everyone who would read her story on the pages of the Bible in the future. Sometimes there's a reason why an answer is given to us that maybe we weren't expecting or that we weren't wanting. Sometimes God has other things in mind for us when we're asking for something in particular. I can't wait for us to begin our study of specific prayers of the Bible, because we're going to see some great examples of this in Scripture.

THE SOLUTION: We need to prepare our hearts through Bible study. When we study Scripture, we come to know the personality of God **more and more**, we come to understand the eternal purpose of God **more and more**, we come to realize the beautiful promises of God **more and more**. As we study the Scripture, we become more familiar with the God we serve and we better understand His nature. Consider these truths: God has complete power, He knows everything, and He is always present. He never changes. God is holy, merciful, gracious, just, sovereign, righteous, and true. He is love. When we come to understand His nature, the doubt obstacle should go away. When we pray, we must remember that it has to be according to God's will, in faith, believing that God is going to answer. And He will.

Prayer Prompt

I'm going to give you a prayer prompt and I urge you to pray about it. I'm taking it from Psalm 62:8. "*Trust in Him at all times, you people; pour out your heart before Him; God is a refuge for us.*" This is a great verse to reflect on when things are hard. We face difficult times in our country, in our communities, and in our homes. Occasionally, we encounter situations that are stressful or uncertain. But this verse says trust in God at all times and pour out your heart before Him. That's prayer: pouring out your heart before God. He is a refuge for us. The word *refuge* here in the Hebrew means "shelter." God is a shelter for us. And I love the word that you find at the end of this verse—*selah*. Selah is interpreted in different ways. Some people believe that it was used as a musical notation, maybe indicating a place to pause. In the original translation of the Septuagint it meant "an intermission." I think this is a wonderful concept! When you see the word selah in Scripture, it should cause you to pause. In other words, stop there and think about what you just read. Go back and reflect on it a little bit deeper. "*Trust in God at all times; pour out your heart before Him; He is your shelter.*" Listen to those words. Pray those words. Pray for God to be a shelter to you, to your family, to your friends, to your country, and to the entire world. When you experience a time of trial, this verse says trust in God. I encourage you to use prayer in order to pour out your heart to Him, believing that He is a shelter to you.

Prayer is important because it is our means of _____ with _____.

It promotes our spiritual _____ and _____.

WHY PRAY?? BECAUSE....

1. God is our _____.

2. We need God's _____.

3. We _____ God.

4. God _____ prayer.

5. It is a form of _____ and _____.

6. It demonstrates our _____.

7. It is a _____ that comes with _____.

8. _____ prayed.

WHAT KEEPS US FROM PRAYING?

1. The _____ obstacle!

Solution: We have to _____.

2. The _____ obstacle!

Solution: We need to _____.

3. The _____ obstacle!

Solution: We must _____ through Bible study.

Prayer Practice

Pour out your heart to God through prayer today. Pray about your worries, your fears, your uncertainties, and your frustrations. Do you have obstacles in your life that keep you from praying? Pray about those, too. Tell God about all of the things that are weighing heavy on your mind, then lay them all down at His feet, and thank Him for being your refuge (Psalm 62:8).

_____

_____

_____

_____

_____

_____

_____

_____

_____

_____

_____

_____

_____

_____

_____

_____

_____

_____

_____

_____

_____

_____

_____

_____

_____

_____

_____

The Practice of Prayer

UNDERSTANDING the reason for prayer is an important first step, but then comes the question of "How?" Many people get stuck right here—knowing **why** they should pray, but not really sure **how** they should pray. In this lesson, we're going to look closely at the practice of prayer. We're going to focus first on how we should pray. We will consider what our responsibility is when it comes to prayer. Then next, I'm going to suggest some practical tips for strengthening our prayer lives that I hope will be very helpful.

How should we pray?

FIRST, WE SHOULD FOLLOW JESUS' EXAMPLE. Just like in everything else that we do, we should look to Christ as our perfect example when it comes to prayer. In Matthew 6:5-13, we read a portion of Scripture that is often referred to as "The Model Prayer." Jesus was preaching on a mountain to His disciples and in this particular moment, He was talking about prayer. Here is what He said:

> And when you pray, you shall not be like the hypocrites, for they love to pray standing in the synagogues and on the corners of the streets that they may be seen by men. Assuredly I say to you, they have their reward. But you, when you pray, go into your room and shut the door and pray to your Father who is in the secret place; and your Father who sees in secret will reward you openly. And when you pray, do not use vain repetitions as the heathen do; for they think that they will be heard for their many words. Therefore do not be like them; for your Father knows the things you have need of before you ask Him.

> In this manner therefore pray, 'Our Father in heaven, hallowed be Your name. Your kingdom

come, Your will be done on earth as it is in heaven. Give us this day our daily bread and forgive us our debts as we forgive our debtors. And do not lead us into temptation, but deliver us from the evil one; for Yours is the kingdom and the power and the glory forever. Amen.'

There are a few lessons to learn from Jesus about prayer in this example that He gave:

1. PRAY SECRETLY. Jesus talked about the hypocrites who loved to stand on the corners of the streets and in the synagogues and pray where they could be seen. They would use many words and draw lots of attention to themselves. Jesus said, "Don't be like that. Don't pray in that way." He said, "Go into your room, shut the door, and pray **in secret**." In other words, prayer is not for show. It's not to bring attention to yourself. In fact, when you are having personal prayer time, when you are having that intimate communion with God in prayer, you should go somewhere where there aren't any distractions. Go to a place where you can have nice, quiet, alone time with God, free from interruption if possible, where you can talk to God by yourself. It's important to find some time during the day when you are able to have one-on-one time with God. That time of fellowship with just you and your Heavenly Father is uplifting and strengthening.

2. PRAY SINCERELY. Jesus talked about how the heathen prayed with vain repetitions, thinking that they were going to be heard because of their many words. He said, "Don't be like that. God already knows what you need. He wants to hear words from your heart, so pray sincerely. Pray authentically." God is not grading our prayers. He's not standing above you thinking, "That was a good one earlier, but this one is not so good." He just wants us to talk to Him, and He wants our words to come from our hearts, from a very real place. When it says to avoid vain repetitions, the key word there is *vain*. The word *vain* is defined as "empty, or meaningless." Don't just say something because you're in the habit of saying it over and over. Understand that it is okay to pray for the same things. There are certain things that we pray for daily: our children, our spouses, our health, our blessings, and much more. I pray about those continually, but I mean it sincerely. Praying repetitiously is not wrong, but what you want to be careful about is using empty, meaningless repetitions—words that don't mean anything. Words that you say simply because it seems like you should say them. Words that have no genuine meaning behind them.

God wants you and me to talk to Him as if we're talking to a friend.

Those are vain repetitions and Jesus warned His disciples about praying in that way. God wants you and me to talk to Him as if we are talking to a friend. I love the words Fanny Crosby wrote in the song "Draw Me Nearer." Listen to these lines: "*Oh the pure delight of a single hour that before Thy throne I spend, when I kneel in prayer, and with Thee, my God, I commune as friend with friend.*" God wants us to have real conversation with Him: heartfelt, authentic words lifted up to Him in prayer.

3. PRAY SPECIFICALLY. In this example, Jesus shows that there are different elements that are incorporated in prayer. Prayer is not simply a list of things that you need: "I need this, I need this, I need this, I need this." Prayer is much more! The ability we have to bring our requests to God is certainly one aspect, but there are others that we should not overlook. If you work your way through this prayer, beginning in verse 9 and on down through verse 15, look at the different components you find! There is praise: "*Our Father in Heaven, hallowed be Your name.*" There is submission: "*Your kingdom come. Your will be done on earth as it is in Heaven. Yours is the kingdom and the power and the glory forever.*" There is supplication (request): "*Give us this day our daily bread. And do not lead us into temptation but deliver us from the evil one.*" There is confession: "*Forgive us our debts as we forgive our debtors.*" Several different elements were covered in this prayer. It's a wonderful example. Prayer is not a shopping list of all the things that we want. It should have other aspects as well. We're going to talk more about that again in the practical application portion of this chapter.

4. PRAY STEADFASTLY. This prayer asks, "*Give us **this day** our **daily bread**.*" Notice that it's a daily prayer. Our prayers involve asking for things that are needed on a daily basis. It makes me think of 1 Thessalonians 5:17. This verse tells us that we should pray without ceasing. In other words, pray continually throughout the day. Remember that prayer can come at any moment, in any form, and that we can pray for anything and everything. I like how the Cambridge English Dictionary defines the word steadfastly as "strongly and without stopping". That's what Paul is saying to the Thessalonians and that's the idea when it comes to daily prayer. Pray strongly and without stopping! We'll also talk more about this in the application section below.

> **Remember that prayer can come at any moment, in any form, and that we can pray for anything and everything.**

When we follow Jesus' example of prayer, especially as it applies to this section of Scripture in Matthew 6, remember: pray secretly, pray sincerely, pray specifically, and pray steadfastly.

SECOND, WE SHOULD PRAY WITH THE RIGHT ATTITUDE. In Luke chapter 18, we read about the parable of the Pharisee and the tax collector. You might be familiar with this account found in verses 9 through 14. Jesus described a scene where two men went up to the temple to pray. One was a Pharisee and the other was a tax collector. The Pharisee stood and began his prayer by saying, "God, I thank you that I am not like other men." From there, he listed some of the people he felt like he was better than—extortioners, unjust, adulterers, and he even called out the tax collector. Then, he mentioned a couple of his great works: "I fast twice a week; I give tithes of all that I possess." But the tax collector, standing far off, wouldn't even lift his eyes to heaven. He beat his hands on his chest and said, "God, be merciful to me; I am a sinner!" There are two very different prayers pictured here. Jesus explained that it was the tax collector who went away justified rather than the Pharisee. He said, *"For everyone who exalts himself will be humbled, and he who humbles himself will be exalted."* Pray in sincerity, in reverence, and in humility. We have to remember whose throne we're approaching and who we are in the presence of God.

THIRD, WE SHOULD PRAY IN FAITH. Simply put, this means that you believe in what you're praying for and who you're praying to. Matthew 21:21-22 talks about having faith and not doubting. Believe, and you will receive. We can't pray and not expect God to answer. We can't pray and doubt His ability to hear and to respond. In his epistle, James wrote, *"If any of you lacks wisdom, let him ask of God, who gives to all liberally and without reproach, and it will be given to him. But let him ask in faith, with no doubting, for he who doubts is like a wave of the sea driven and tossed by the wind. For let not that man suppose that he will receive anything from the Lord; he is a double-minded man, unstable in all his ways"* (James 1:5-8). To "ask in faith" is trusting and relying on God to answer. The word doubting in this context is translated from the Greek word *diakrino,* literally meaning "to judge back and forth." It's the idea of having an internal debate or changing from one idea to another. It's a picture of confusion and instability, James said, like waves of the sea being tossed in every direction by the wind or a man having two different minds. To pray with doubt is to believe on one hand that God is going to answer the prayer, but on the other hand believe that He won't. To pray in faith is to know that God is there, to believe that He is hearing every word, to trust that He has the power to answer, and to have confidence that He will do what is best for you.

FOURTH, WE SHOULD PRAY WITH UNDERSTANDING. We have to know the limitations of prayer and the will of God. We can't ask God for something that would require Him to go against His own will. We can't ask for something that is against His commands or against the instruction that He has given us in His Word. We can't ask for something that would be in direct opposition to what He has told us or what He has revealed to us in Scripture. He's not going to violate His own will in order to satisfy man. And we shouldn't expect Him to! His will is good and perfect and acceptable. In Matthew 6:9, mentioned earlier, remember the words in that prayer: *"Your will be done.* **Your** *will be done."* We have to pray with understanding. Part of that involves understanding that God's providence is going to prevail. Romans 8:28 is a wonderful verse that talks about how all things are going to work together for good for those who love the Lord and who are called according to His purpose. That doesn't mean that terrible things happen in order to result in something good. There are some things that happen, and you might say, "Look at what a great thing happened as a result of that." But there are also some things that happen, and you might not be able to say that at all. The promise is God is always working in our lives and that He can take things that happen and use them in a way that will work together for good and will ultimately bring glory to Him. Some things I don't know that we'll ever really understand until we're in Heaven one day, but we have to know that God's providence is working, that He can redeem any situation, that He can redeem any person. We have to understand and believe that when we talk to Him in prayer.

FINALLY, WE SHOULD PRAY THROUGH CHRIST. The avenue to God is through Christ. In John 14:6, Jesus said, "*No man comes to the Father but by Me.*" We can also reflect on Jesus' teaching in John 14:12-14. "*Most assuredly I say to you, he who believes in Me, the works that I do he will do also; and greater works than these he will do, because I go to My Father. And whatever you ask in My name, that I will do, that the Father may be glorified in the Son. If you ask anything in My name, I will do it.*" Notice how Jesus said that twice. "*Whatever you ask in My name, I will do it.*" It is important that we pray through Jesus—in His name.

These are five things to think about when it comes to our responsibility in prayer. But, now let's get practical. What can we do in real, everyday life in order to improve our praying habits? Here are what I call:

Practical Tips for Praying Lips

1. BE STILL.

We need to slow down. Sometimes we have to take a minute to stop and just breathe. It's easy to rush, rush, rush, trying to get everything on our to-do list checked off; and if we're not careful, we can bump prayer right off the list and out of our day. The truth is, if you and I don't have time to pray, then we're too busy. We need to look at all of the things we have going on in our lives and say, "If I don't have time during my day to stop and to talk to my Heavenly Father, then I need to look at my schedule and evaluate where my time is going!" Sometimes it takes slowing down and being still in order to give our time and attention to prayer.

Sometimes it takes slowing down and being still in order to give our time and attention to prayer.

2. STAY ORGANIZED.

How in the world can staying organized help your prayer life? (I know some of you non-list makers are screaming, "Noooooooo!"—but hang on! You can do this!) If you think ahead and do a little pre-planning, then your prayer time can be much better managed.

    a. First, thanks to technology, there are many different programs that you can use to help you stay organized in this area of your life. There are a variety of prayer apps available to download on your phone, your iPad, your laptop, whatever it is that you use. These apps can help you keep track of prayer requests, schedule prayer time, access Scriptures to read and meditate on, and some even offer Bible stories that are read out loud. You can have notifications that remind you to pray. When you hear the chime, it's time to take some time to stop and pray.

b. You can also use a prayer journal to write down your prayers. Here is an idea that I really love: Keep a little notebook next to your computer or to have on hand—in the car or in a purse. Then, when you are breezing through email, Facebook, Twitter, Instagram, or any other form of social media and you see prayer requests from your friends or family, you can use your notebook for keeping a list of those requests. Then in your prayer time, you can pull out your notebook and make sure that you lift up those names and situations to God. Because a lot of times we'll tell people that we are praying for them and we want to make sure that when we say that, we really are bringing their request to God in prayer.

c. Try different methods of praying. For example, try using the ACTS prayer. This acronym stands for: adoration, confession, thanksgiving, and supplication. It's a good way to keep your thoughts on track in prayer. And, of course, you can always go back to the five-finger prayer that we teach children when they are young. In this prayer, your fingers remind you to pray for certain people. First, put your hands palm to palm in front of you. Then, you start with your thumbs and work through your fingers all the way to your pinkies. The thumb reminds you to pray for those closest to you, the pointer is for those in authority, the middle finger is for our leaders, the ring finger is for those who are weak, and the pinky reminds you to pray for yourself. You can do an internet search to find this prayer explained in much more detail. It's wonderful for children, but it is just as wonderful for adults who sometimes struggle with what to say in prayer. You might also try a theme prayer, like a "room" prayer or a "days-of-the-week" prayer. A room prayer involves walking from room to room in your house and praying for the people who stay there and for the activities that take place in each room. A days-of-the-week prayer assigns a specific prayer focus for each day of the week. For example, Sunday—the church, Monday—family, Tuesday—friends, and so on. That doesn't mean you can't pray for those subjects on other days, but you remember them specifically on those days. I know that my mother prays for me all the time, but I love that Tuesday is **my** day! On Tuesdays I know that she is lifting up my name in a focused and intentional prayer on my behalf. *(I love you, Mom!)*

d. You can also schedule prayer time as you are working on creating prayer habits. Take a look at your daily planner. Where do you have time that you can spend a portion of time with God specifically? Block off time where you are able to remain free from work, school, appointments, phone calls, and other interruptions so that you can be alone with God in prayer. This might be early in the morning, late at night, or at any point during the day. If you don't have any free time from the time you wake up until you crawl into bed at night, then take just a second to go back and read #1 again! You might be too busy, or you might need to ask someone for help. There is no question that this becomes even more challenging when you have young children, but let me encourage you to find ways to make it happen. You might have to get creative! Give scheduled prayer time a try. It will help you create a prayer habit that will truly bless your life.

e. It might be helpful for you to find a prayer partner or a prayer group. This is a person, or several people, who will hold you accountable and encourage you in your prayer life— and you will do the same for her (or for them). Being a part of a small prayer group of Christian sisters has had a powerful influence on my life. Those precious ladies are a great source of comfort and support for me. We share each other's burdens and blessings, pray for each other regularly, and love each other fiercely!

3. REMAIN FOCUSED.

Sometimes it is difficult to stay focused when we are praying. Remember the first point we talked about when it comes to how we should pray? **Pray secretly**. I would suggest that you think about having a praying place. Quite literally, a place where you go to pray. I have a place where I sit every morning. I get up way before everybody else, I drink my coffee, I have my Bible reading and devotional time, and that's also when I talk to God in prayer. I look forward to that personal time every single day. If everyone is awake and I need to get away to a quiet place, I go to my closet, shut the door, and I'll pray in my closet for a while. Have a place where you go, where it's easier for you to think and to focus on your words. Somebody also told me one time that it's a good idea to pray for your distractions. Whatever your distractions are when you are trying to pray, pray about those things or for those people. Maybe your distractions are your children. Pray for them right in that moment. If it's work, then pray about that. Pray for the things that distract you from your time spent in prayer.

4. FIND TIME TO PRAY IN UNIQUE PLACES.

I just talked about getting up early. Sometimes, Jesus got up while it was still dark, or He prayed at night when he could be alone. Pray when you're in the car. Some of you, if you commute to work or school, have a great opportunity to have some conversation time with God while you're driving.

When my children are in the car with me, we sing, we laugh, we talk about big things and little things, and we pray. You can pray while you're exercising, while you're walking or jogging on that treadmill, or while you're taking a walk or running in the neighborhood. One time, I had a friend tell me that she prays while she's ironing, folding clothes, washing dishes, or while she's doing other things around the house. She uses those moments, those unique places, as her time to pray.

To teach kids to pray is to teach them one of the most effective strategies for fighting evil in this world.

5. TEACH KIDS TO PRAY.

This is really powerful, because really what you are doing is training children for spiritual battle. You are teaching them one of the most effective strategies for fighting evil in this world. But what you may not realize is that while you're teaching them to pray, you are also benefiting—you are teaching yourself how to pray. You can take the pointers that you're giving them, and you can apply them to your own life. You know, when you teach anything (and I'm sure some of you have heard this or even said it before) you as the teacher sometimes grow even more than the students. That's true with prayer, too. As you train your children how to pray, you are growing from that as well. Also, let your children hear you pray. Let them know that it's important to you to have time to talk to God. Your example is helping them learn how to become faithful stewards of prayer.

6. BE GENUINE.

A genuine person is one who is exactly what she appears to be. She is true. She is real. She is not trying to imitate someone else. She speaks her feelings from her own heart. Be genuine when you pray. Talk to God as if He were right there with you, because He actually is right there with you! Talk to Him like you're talking to a friend, but not in a flippant or disrespectful way. Speak reverently to your Almighty Creator, but also whole-heartedly and authentically. The more time you spend with God in prayer, the more at ease you will feel talking to Him about your struggles, your dreams, your temptations, your fears, and your worries. You will build a relationship based on honesty and trust, and you will discover that time spent in prayer with God is also time spent confiding in a friend.

7. AVOID REDUNDANT WORDS.

Redundant words are unnecessary, repetitious words. They are words that are needless or useless. You might be using them because it just sounds like you should use them. We want to try to avoid that, because this comes back to the point about being genuine. We want to make sure that our words are meaningful. Sometimes to avoid redundant words in our prayers, we might have to do some prayer exercises. If you struggle with words, one of the things that you can do is pray the psalms. That's a wonderful exercise! Go through the book of Psalms and find one with a theme that fits whatever it is that you have on your heart. Maybe it is a praise psalm, maybe it is a psalm of confession, maybe it is a psalm of asking for forgiveness, or maybe it's a psalm asking for strength. It's very easy to do a search for the themes of the psalms on the internet. Choose one that captures what is on your heart, then turn to that psalm in the Bible and speak the words in the form of a prayer. Use the words given by the Holy Spirit. That is not using vain repetitions; that is finding a way to express what you're feeling. It can be a very effective prayer exercise. Something else you can try is to write out a prayer in the form of a note or a letter. If you have something that you want to talk to God about and you can't find the words to pray, sometimes you might be able to find the words to write. This can be a note of thanks, a note of confession, a note of praise, any type of note that allows you to express in written words what you would like to say in prayer to God.

> *The more time you spend with God in prayer, the more at ease you will feel talking to Him about your struggles, your dreams, your temptations, your fears, and your worries.*

8. DON'T BE TOO HARD ON YOURSELF.

Prayer is big. It is a grand privilege. It is not a small thing. Prayer is coming into the presence of our Almighty God and talking to Him. That is beautiful, and it's big. So, if you're struggling to feel stronger, more confident about it, don't be too hard on yourself. It's okay. Give yourself some grace. Just don't abandon it. It is too big a part of your spiritual life to not give it the attention that it needs. Keep doing it. Keep working every day to strengthen your prayer life, because there is nothing, **nothing** that is better, that is more encouraging, that is more strength-building than coming into the presence of God and talking to Him. Remember, He is your power source.

 **Prayer Prompt**

My prayer prompt for you today is to pray using the ACTS format: adoration, confession, thanksgiving, and supplication. Try to incorporate each one of those elements into your prayer. Keep Philippians 4:6 in mind: "*Be anxious for nothing, but in everything by prayer and supplication, with thanksgiving, let your requests be made known to God.*" Remember that supplication means humbly asking for what it is that we need, and thanksgiving is doing it with a spirit of gratitude. Today, in at least one of your prayers, try to pray each of those different elements. Adoration is referring to praise for God. Confession is concerning whatever you are struggling with at this particular time. This might be a place in your prayer for repentance or to ask for forgiveness. Thanksgiving is expressing gratitude for the blessings in your life. Finally, supplication is a time to talk about the things that are on your heart, the needs that you might have, or what you would like to pray for other people.

HOW SHOULD WE PRAY?

1. Follow Jesus' _____ of prayer.

    A. Consider how He taught His disciples to pray (Matthew 6:5-13).

        a. Pray _____.

   b.   Pray _____.

   c.   Pray _____.

   d.   Pray _____ .

2. With the _____ _____.

3. In _____.

4. With _____.

5. Through _____.

PRACTICAL TIPS FOR PRAYING LIPS:

1. Be _____!

2. Stay _____.

3. Remain _____.

4. Find time in _____ places.

5. Teach _____ to pray.

6. Be _____.

7. Avoid _____ words.

8. Don't be too _____ on _____.

Prayer Practice

Try to pray using the ACTS acronym (Adoration, Confession, Thanksgiving, and Supplication). First, praise God. Then, talk to Him about your personal struggles. Next, thank Him for how He has blessed you. Finally, ask Him for those things that are on your heart.

_____

_____

_____

_____

_____

_____

_____

_____

O Lord of hosts, if You will indeed look on the affliction of Your maidservant, but will give Your maidservant a male child, then I will give him to the Lord all the days of his life, and no razor shall come upon his head.

1 SAMUEL 1:11

Prayer One

1 SAMUEL 1:11

The Prayer

A woman named Hannah spoke the words of this prayer in anguish and desperation as she begged God for a son.

Previously...

As we begin to look deeper into the prayer of Hannah, it's important to remember that in Israelite history her story takes place between the period of the judges and the period of the kings. As 1 Samuel is beginning, the period of the judges is coming to an end, and in just a few chapters, the Israelites are going to be crying out for a king so that they can be like other nations. When we meet Hannah in Scripture, the kings have not started to reign—we've not yet met Saul—but that time is drawing near.

In the first verse of 1 Samuel, we meet some of the key people in this story about Hannah. We meet her husband Elkanah, and in the second verse we are told that Elkanah had two wives. Hannah was his wife and he also had a wife named Peninnah. We learn something else very important in verse 2 about these two women. We find out that Peninnah had children, but that Hannah did not have any children—an important detail to keep in mind throughout this story. As we move along in the chapter, we find out that Elkanah makes a yearly journey up to the tabernacle in order to make a sacrifice, and he takes his family with him. It says in verse 4, that when the time came for Elkanah to make an offering, he would give portions to Peninnah and all of her sons and daughters. Then in verse 5, we learn that he would give double portions to Hannah, because it says that "he loved her." But, we also Elkanah loved Hannah, the text continues on to say, "Although the Lord had closed her womb." We know from verse 2 that she doesn't have any children and then in verse 5 we are told the reason why.

In the next two verses we learn something else very important in this story. We discover how Peninnah treated Hannah. Remember, Peninnah is the other wife and she had sons and daughters. In verse 6 it refers to Peninnah as Hannah's rival and explains that she "provoked her severely." The Hebrew word that is translated "provoke" means "to vex." In the *Merriam-Webster Dictionary* the definition of vex is "to bring trouble, distress, or agitation to." The word severely in the Hebrew text emphasizes the extent to which Peninnah provoked Hannah. We're not told specifically what she does to provoke her, maybe she insulted her or made fun of her; but we do know that her intent was to make Hannah miserable. The word translated *miserable* in the Hebrew text is an interesting word. It's the word *raam*, meaning "to thunder." Peninnah's agitation of Hannah was so intense that it caused Hannah "to thunder." Think of the rumbling and shaking that is caused by thunder and the fear and anxiety that often results. The use of the word here is to describe that it brought Hannah trouble, fret, and irritation. We also know that, according to verse 7, "it happened year by year" when they went up to the house of the Lord to worship and sacrifice. This was an ongoing occurrence and it grieved Hannah to the point that she wept and didn't eat.

What does it mean to "pour out your soul" before the Lord?

Then, look at Elkanah's response to her in verse 8. It says that Elkanah her husband asked her, "Hannah, why are you crying? Why are you not eating? Why is your heart grieved? Am I not better to you than ten sons?" He showed his concern for her, but he just doesn't seem to understand what Hannah was feeling; he couldn't truly empathize. So, in verse 9, we are told that Hannah arose after they had finished eating and drinking in Shiloh and went to pray. At the same time, Eli the priest was sitting on the seat by the doorpost of the tabernacle. Hannah is described in verse 10 as being in "bitterness of soul" and as she prayed to the Lord she was in anguish and crying. Bitterness is caused by or an expression of severe pain, grief, or regret (*Merriam-Webster Dictionary*). The Hebrew word for *bitterness* there is *marat*, similar to the name Naomi gave herself—*Mara*—because she said that the Lord had dealt very bitterly with her, having lost her husband and both of her sons (Ruth 1:20).

And this is where we reach Hannah's prayer in verse 11. She lifted up these words to the Lord, "*O Lord of hosts, if You will indeed look on the affliction of Your maidservant, but will give Your maidservant a male child, then I will give him to the Lord all the days of his life, and no razor shall come upon his head.*" And as she prayed, Eli watched her. His first thought was that she had had too much to drink! He believes that she is intoxicated, because verse 13 says Hannah "spoke in her heart, and her lips moved, but her voice was not heard." In other words, she mouthed the words of her prayer. And, remember the verse just before says that she wept in anguish. That phrase "wept in anguish" is from the Hebrew word *bakah*, also defined as "bewail," which means "to express deep sorrow for something usually by wailing and lamentation."

Imagine the scene from Eli's perspective: a woman, alone, mouthing words and crying out loudly in her pain and sadness. She may have been on her knees on the ground, maybe lifting her hands to Heaven or maybe using them to cover her face. She might have been rocking back and forth in anguish or shaking with emotion. We can only imagine, but it is to the point that Eli approached her and asked, "How long will you be drunk? Put your wine away from you." Hannah explained herself to him by saying, "No, I am a woman of sorrowful spirit. I have drunk neither wine nor intoxicating drink, but I've poured out my soul before the Lord. Do not consider your maidservant a wicked woman; for out of the abundance of my complaint and grief I have spoken until now."

The Purpose

What was the purpose of Hannah's prayer? Why did she pray the prayer we find in verse 11? The reason was that she wanted a son. That was the request she made of God in her prayer: "*Give Your maidservant a male child.*" Do you think that was the first time she had brought that particular prayer before God? Do you think the words we read in verse 11 were spoken by Hannah for the first and only time in that one moment? I don't think so. I don't think that was the first prayer that she had ever lifted up to God about her desire to have a child. We don't know how long Hannah had been praying for a son. We do know from verse 7 that Hannah endured insulting and mocking from Peninnah "year by year when she went up to the house of the Lord," which would cause her to cry and stop eating. Then, in verse 10, Hannah had reached the point of anguish and bitterness of soul. Her heart was in a state of grief. This was clearly something that had been troubling Hannah for a while.

And God Said...

How did God answer her prayer? Let's pick up where we left off in Hannah's story. She had just explained to Eli that she was not drunk, but that she had been praying. Beginning in verse 17: "Then Eli answered and said to her, 'Go in peace, and the God of Israel grant your petition which you have asked of Him.' And she said, 'Let your maidservant find favor in your sight.' So the woman went her way and ate, and her face was no longer sad." Eli's words brought Hannah's heart some degree of contentment. It may have been that Eli was praying with her, asking God to grant her petition, or it may have been that Eli spoke those words as a prophecy, saying to Hannah that God would indeed grant her what she had asked of Him. Whichever it was, Hannah went away and she was no longer sad.

The text says that early the next morning, after worshiping the Lord, Elkanah and his family returned to their home. In verse 19 we are told that Elkanah knew Hannah his wife, and the Lord remembered her. Then, in the process of time, Hannah conceived and gave birth to a son. She called him Samuel and said she had chosen that name "because I have asked for him from the Lord." Hannah was blessed with a child. Her prayer was answered. God gave her the gift of a son. In Hebrew, the name *Samuel* literally means "name of God" or "heard of God."

God's answer is always the right one and it always comes at the right time.

In verses 21 and 22, we read that Elkanah took his family up for the yearly sacrifice, but Hannah did not join them. Her plan was to wait until Samuel was old enough to be weaned and then she would make the trip with him to Shiloh. Hannah's words were, "Not until the child is weaned; then I will take him, that he may appear before the Lord and remain there forever." She had not forgotten her promise. She remembered the vow she made to God. Back in verse 11 her prayer was "give your maidservant a male child, then I will give him to the Lord all the days of his life...." Essentially, "Lord, if you give me what I'm asking—if you will give me a son—then, I will give him back to you." And that's exactly what Hannah did.

When Hannah brought Samuel to Eli these were the words of obedience, love, and faithfulness that she spoke to him, "O my lord! As your soul lives, my lord, I am the woman who stood by you here praying to the Lord. For this child I prayed, and the Lord has granted me my petition which I asked of Him. Therefore I also have lent him to the Lord; as long as he lives he shall be lent to the Lord." What a beautiful example Hannah is to us even today.

Why do you think God answered her request and why do you think it took as long as it did? Remember, it was probably not the only time that Hannah had prayed that specific prayer. It was probably not the first time that she asked God for a son. But, she was at a place in her heart where she was so grieved and she so desperately wanted a child that she prayed a promise that she may not have prayed a year before, or two years before, or however many years before. Hannah had to arrive at a place where she was willing to pray a prayer that said: "If you will answer my prayer, Lord, if you will give me the child that I so desperately want, I will give him back to you." I don't know that she would have prayed a prayer offering her son back to the Lord if it had been earlier, if it had been her first time she prayed for a son or the second time she prayed for a son or the third or the fourth or the fifth, or on and on and on. She had to come to the point of almost praying in desperation, "Give me a son and I will give him to You." She had to get there. And God knew she had to get there. His timing is at work in Hannah's life, from the words "the Lord had closed her womb" to "the Lord remembered her" to "the Lord has granted me my petition which I asked of Him." God's answer is always the right one and it always comes at the right time.

And look what God accomplished through the life of Samuel! He became a priest. He became a prophet. He became a judge. He became a faithful leader in Israel. He was a true servant of God and the people looked up to him and respected him. He was the one who anointed the head of Saul, and then he was the one that anointed the head of God's chosen king, David. He was a figure of authority, referred to in Jeremiah 15:1 and Psalm 99:6 for his devotion to God. Just look at the great way that God used Hannah's son Samuel: all because Hannah was willing to give back to God what He so graciously gave to her.

In chapter 2 of 1 Samuel, we read Hannah's prayer of praise. She has just given up her only son and the first words of her prayer were, *"My heart rejoices in the Lord."* Her prayer was powerful! She spoke of the Lord's strength, knowledge, and judgment. When I read her prayer, I don't picture it coming from a weak or timid woman; I picture it coming from a woman of courage and tenacity. The Bible goes on to tell us that Hannah had more children. She was blessed with three more sons and two daughters. 2 Samuel 2:21 ends by saying, *"Meanwhile the child Samuel grew before the Lord."*

The Present

Hannah's story is an amazing one. It teaches us that God is purposeful, that times of waiting might be part of a plan that God has for us, and that those times of waiting can actually result in enormous blessing. We learn that in times of desperation, in times of sorrow, we should go to God in prayer; we should pray and talk to him about what is on our heart, and He will listen. When it comes to your own personal prayer life, never forget this: God always listens. When you are in a time of waiting, when you feel like you're not getting an answer, when you feel like you have asked and you have asked and you have asked and still nothing is happening—remember that something **is** happening. The answer might be "wait." God might be saying "I need for you to wait because I am working on something, and it is going to be a tremendous blessing; but I need you to be patient because it's going to happen in My perfect time."

In Hannah's case, Hannah had to get to a point of being willing to give what she wanted most back to God. When she got to that point, God said "All right. Now, **now**, I'm ready to answer your prayer, because now you're in the right frame of mind and the orientation of your heart is right. **Now**, I'm ready to do great things through you." It's a wonderful lesson about what we should know when we feel like God's not listening. It's a wonderful example of what happens when we wait on God.

Another amazing way that prayers in waiting can be a blessing is by building the faith of others. When my sister and her husband were ready to start a family, they encountered some challenges with infertility. They desperately wanted children and our entire family kept them in prayer asking specifically for God to bless them with a child. Every night, my children talked to God about their aunt and uncle and prayed that they would be able to have a baby. Time passed and we were all excited when they began to talk about adoption. Then, one day we got the call that there was a baby coming, but not in the way we were anticipating. My sister had discovered she was pregnant. When she and my brother-in-law told my children the news, they were ecstatic! Their bedtime prayers were drenched with joy and happy "thank you"s! It was a good lesson for our entire family about the blessings that come from waiting on God. Even if the situation had a different ending—a precious child through adoption, or another path completely—the prayers that had been offered for so long by so many had not fallen on the ears of an unhearing Father.

 *Prayer Prompt*

Today's prayer prompt comes from Isaiah 30:18 and has to do with this idea of waiting. Isaiah 30:18 says, "Therefore the Lord will wait, that He may be gracious to you; and therefore He will be exalted, that He may have mercy on you; for the Lord is the God of justice. Blessed are all those who wait for Him." Read that again and think about Hannah.

In your prayer today, I encourage you to specifically think about something that you're waiting for. Maybe something that you have been praying about that you haven't received an answer for, or maybe something for which you've prayed and prayed and prayed and you've questioned whether God is listening. Think about that thing, whatever that might be, and in your prayer, when you pray about that today, ask God to help you find comfort in knowing that He hears you. In your prayer, thank Him for working in your life even when you can't see it. Because He is! Try to say those words in some way, in some form in your prayer. That is a prayer of faith.

If you have a situation where you are waiting on an answer; there's something that has been on your heart and you've prayed about it over and over and you're wondering when and how God is going to work, let me give you some Scripture references to meditate on. These verses all have to do with waiting on God: Psalm 25:4-5; Psalm 27:13-14; Psalm 33:20-22; Psalm 37:7, 9; Psalm 40:1-3; Psalm 62:5; Isaiah 40:29-31; Isaiah 64:4; Lamentations 3:25; and Micah 7:7. In your personal devotional time, if it would be helpful for you, read these verses and be encouraged by what the Bible says about God's perfect timing.

O Lord of hosts, if You will indeed look on the affliction of Your maidservant, but will give Your maidservant a male child, then I will give him to the Lord all the days of his life, and no razor shall come upon his head.

1 SAMUEL 1:11

1. Who was praying in this Scripture reference and what were the circumstances leading up to this moment?

2. What was the purpose of this prayer?

3. Do you think this was the first time this person had brought this particular prayer before God? Why or why not?

4. How did God answer?

5. Why do you think He answered in the way—and in the time frame—that He did?

6. What do we learn from this prayer that we can apply to our personal prayer lives?

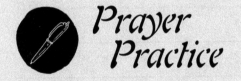 **Prayer Practice**

Is there a prayer that you have been waiting for God to answer? Today when you pray, ask God for comfort in knowing that He hears you, and thank Him for working for your good and for His glory even when it's hard for you to see. Ask God to strengthen your faith and fill you with joy during this time of waiting as you are "praying through it"! Reflect on the words of Isaiah 30:18 and remember that the Lord will wait so that He may be gracious to you.

_____

_____

_____

_____

_____

_____

_____

O Lord God, remember me, I pray! Strengthen me, I pray just this once, O God, that I may with one blow take vengeance on the Philistines for my two eyes.

JUDGES 16:28

Prayer Two

JUDGES 16:28

The Prayer

These words were lifted up to God from the mouth of Samson, a judge of Israel, as a desperate cry for a measure of strength.

Previously...

If we go back just a few chapters, we will find the beginning of this story. Judges 13 is where the prophecy of the birth of a man named Samson takes place. His father, Manoah, was married to a woman who was not able to have children. In verse 3 of chapter 13, the Angel of the Lord appeared to Manoah's wife and said to her, *"Indeed now, you are barren and have borne no children, but you shall conceive and bear a son. Now therefore, please be careful not to drink wine or similar drink, and not to eat anything unclean. For behold, you shall conceive and bear a son. And no razor shall come upon his head, for the child shall be a Nazarite to God from the womb; and he shall begin to deliver Israel out of the hand of the Philistines."* The message from the Angel of the Lord to

Manoah's wife was "You're going to have a son," but he followed that up with specific instructions. He told her that the child would be a Nazarite from birth. That meant that her son would be consecrated to God. In other words, he would be distinguished from others for the purpose of accomplishing God's work. It's interesting that in the Bible there are occasions when individuals take a Nazarite vow for a period of time while there are others who are Nazarites from birth and honor the vow for a lifetime. Samson fell into the latter group and would live the life of a Nazarite. There were three parts of the Nazarite vow: They did not cut their hair, they avoided contact with the dead, and they abstained from strong or intoxicating drinks. Not only did Manoah's wife learn that she would have a son and that he would be a Nazarite, but the Angel of the Lord also told her that he was going to deliver the Israelites out of the hand of the Philistines. Her son Samson was going to be a judge for the nation of Israel and that's where his story begins.

His story carries through the next few chapters, and it is an amazing story. It's full of action, adventure, deception, and war. It's frustrating at times and shocking at times! Even more, when you read the story of Samson, you see clearly how God can take people who are very broken and use them to accomplish His will. Samson time and again made choices that cause you to shake your head and think, "Oh, please don't. Please don't do that, Samson!" But, God continued to redeem his situation and used him to bring glory to His name and ultimately to help the Israelite nation. There are ups and downs throughout his story, and the details are intriguing, so I encourage you to go back and spend some time reading Samson's story. We're going to jump ahead to the point where Samson, through a series of events that occurred, was able to defeat the Philistines.

In chapter 16 we find that Samson loved a woman named Delilah. Delilah is set up with a bribe from the Philistines in order to find the source of Samson's strength. Essentially, in verse 5 they said, "If you can find out what the source of Samson's strength is, then each of us will give you money." So, Delilah began to deceive Samson in order to find out the source of his strength. He tricked her a number of times by pretending to tell her the source, only for her to find out later that he had lied to her. Over time she wore him out with her continual asking. She drove him crazy with her persistence. In fact, it says in verse 16 of chapter 16, that *"she pestered him daily with her words and pressed him so that his soul was vexed to death."* He had just had enough! In verse 17 it says, *"He finally told her all his heart and said to her, 'No razor has ever come upon my head, for I have been a Nazarite to God from my mother's womb. If I am shaven, then my strength will leave me, and I shall become weak and be like any other man.'"* Samson finally confessed to her what would have to happen for him to lose his strength. Of course it wasn't really his hair that was the source of his strength, it was the Nazarite vow. When the vow was broken and his head was shaven, then his strength was lost, and he was easily overtaken by the Philistines, who were waiting close by for Delilah to carry through her part of the deception. In verse 21 we read that the Philistines came in and took him. They removed his eyes, bound him with bronze fetters, and he became a grinder in the prison. Samson, the mighty judge and warrior for Israel, was blinded, chained, and made a slave.

At the end of chapter 16, the Philistines were having a feast. They were all gathered together to offer a sacrifice and praises to their god Dagon. Verse 25 says that when their hearts were merry they decided to call for Samson to perform for them. The word *perform* is translated from the Greek word *sachaq*, meaning to "amuse." They wanted to be entertained by Samson in order to make fun of him. They positioned him between two pillars and the Bible says he performed for them. How humiliating that had to have been for Samson! In verse 26, Samson made a request of the boy who was holding his hand, "Let me feel the pillars which support the temple, so that I can lean on them." This paints an even clearer picture of Samson's lack of strength as he was being led by the hand of a child. The next verse says that the temple was full of men and women, all the lords of the Philistines were there, about three thousand men and women on the roof, who watched while Samson performed. The boy guided Samson to the pillars that were holding up the temple. As Samson used the pillars to lean on, he began to pray. He called out to the Lord and said, "*O Lord God, remember me, I pray; strengthen me, pray, just this once, O God, that I may with one blow take vengeance on the Philistines for my two eyes.*"

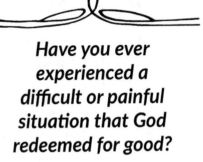

Have you ever experienced a difficult or painful situation that God redeemed for good?

The Purpose

The purpose of this prayer was to request strength. Samson asked God to grant him strength, right in that moment, in order for something specific to happen. Samson was no longer a man of unmatched strength. With the breaking of his Nazarite vow, he had become like other men. In his frailty, his eyes were gouged out and he was forced into chains. When Samson raised up this prayer to God, his desire was to be granted a measure of strength just one more time so that he could avenge himself on the Philistines. He knew that strength could never come from within himself: it could only come from God.

As he stood between the two pillars of the temple where the Philistines were gathered, he must have felt defeated. He had been forced to perform for his enemies—a subject of entertainment in the middle of his suffering. It had to have been humiliating: a once unstoppable, untouchable, unbeatable hero of a man, now blind, broken, and being led by a child to be mocked in front of a crowd. He called out to God to remember him and to replace his weakness with strength so that with one mighty push against the pillars, he could bring the temple to the ground.

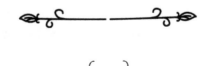

And God Said...

God's answer to Samson's prayer can be found in the next two verses. Samson took hold of the two middle pillars which supported the temple, and he braced himself against them, one on his right and the other on his left. Then Samson said, "Let me die with the Philistines!" He pushed with all his might, and the temple fell on the lords and all the people who were in it. The Bible says that the dead that he killed at his death were more than he had killed in his life. The answer to the prayer was "yes"! God said, "Yes, I will grant you the strength that you are asking for at this moment."

I want to pause here for just a second. Let's shift gears a little bit and look at a story that is found in the book of Genesis. Keep a bookmark in Judges 16, but then flip in your Bible over to Genesis 24. We're going to look at verses 12 through 14. Something similar happened here. Not at all the same situation, but the same type of prayer. Beginning in Genesis 24:12 we read, "*Then he said, 'O Lord God of my master Abraham, please give me success this day, and show kindness to my master Abraham.'*" The person who is praying here is a servant of Abraham who had been sent on a very specific mission. He had been sent by Abraham to his home country and his own family to find a wife for his son Isaac. In fact, Abraham asked him to swear by the Lord God of Heaven that he would carry out that task. He had also told him that if a wife was not willing to follow him, then he would be released from the oath, but that he should not take Isaac back there (verses 1-9). Abraham's servant took the oath and made the journey to Mesopotamia, to the city of Nahor.

In the evening, just outside the city of Nahor, Abraham's servant made his camels kneel by a well in the evening. This was strategic timing, because in verse 11 we find that this was the time of day when the women would go out to draw water. The servant had selected the right place to be at the right time. Certainly, the providence of God was at work! It was at that point that the servant began to pray the words we just read in verse 12. His prayer continues through verses 13 and 14: "*Behold, here I stand by the well of water, and the daughters of the men of the city are coming out to draw water. Now let it be that the young woman to whom I say, 'Please let down your pitcher that I may drink,' and she says, 'Drink, and I will also give your camels a drink'—let her be the one You have appointed for your servant Isaac. And by this I will know that You have shown kindness to my master.*"

This was a prayer that was lifted up when something was needed in the present moment. Abraham's servant had a specific request at that specific time. This is the similarity that we can draw between the prayer that Samson prayed in chapter 16 of Judges and this prayer being prayed in chapter 24 of Genesis by Abraham's servant. Both of these men needed something in the situation at hand. Samson needed strength. Abraham's servant needed guidance. What happened in Genesis 24? What was God's answer? If you keep reading through the story, in verse 15 it says, "*And it happened, before he had finished speaking, that behold, Rebekah, who was born to Bethuel, son of Milcah, the wife of Nahor, Abraham's brother, came out with her pitcher on her shoulder. Now the young woman was very beautiful to behold, a virgin, no man had known her; and she*" *went down to the well, filled her pitcher, and came up.*" Rebekah offered Abraham's servant a drink and then offered to draw water for his camels as well. With that, the servant knew that God had heard and answered his prayer. The story continues with the servant going to the home of Rebekah's father and explaining what had brought him to their country and how God had answered his prayer at the well. Rebekah was given to Isaac as a wife and she returned with Abraham's servant to the land of Canaan.

Samson's name is mentioned in Hebrews 11, among other heroes of faith. Beginning in verse 32, it says, "*And what more shall I say? For the time would fail me to tell of Gideon and Barak, and Samson, and Jephthah, also of David and Samuel and the prophets: who through faith subdued kingdoms, worked righteousness, obtained promises, stopped the mouths of lions, quenched the violence of fire, escaped the edge of the sword, **out of weakness were made strong**, became valiant in battle, turned to flight the armies of the aliens*" (emp. added). Samson is remembered for believing that God could and would give him the strength he needed to overcome his enemies in a state of utter weakness.

The Present

What can we learn from these prayers? Let's first start by asking the question: Would these specific prayers be offered as part of a daily prayer regimen? Is the prayer that Samson prayed in Judges 16:28 one that he prayed daily? No, of course not! That prayer was for a specific request at a specific moment of time. The same was true with the prayer of Abraham's servant. His prayer in Genesis 24:12-14 was not a prayer he offered daily. It was prayed in a unique situation when he needed God's immediate help and guidance. What does that teach us that we can apply to our own prayer lives?

These prayers teach us something extraordinary. They teach us that we can pray at any time, at any moment, for anything. In talking about the subject of prayer and discussing Samson's story, I refer to his prayer in Judges 16:28 as a prayer for STAN. S-T-A-N stands for "Strength To Act Now." A prayer for STAN is a prayer that you pray because you need help "right now." God works our lives providentially. He works in ways that we don't always understand, that we may not fully grasp. But I'll tell you this, when you are in a moment where you need help and you need strength, my first recommendation for you is to take whatever is going on in that moment and immediately take it to God in prayer. When you are faced with something that is difficult, challenging, that you are uncertain about, right then, in that very moment take whatever it is that you are facing and lift it up to God. Ask Him for courage, guidance, help, wisdom; ask for God to help you in that moment with the strength to act now!

On my first medical mission trip in 1996, I traveled with a group of Christians from Abilene, Texas, to Victoria, Mexico. It was a whole new experience for me, and I was beyond excited about helping the people of that city—physically and spiritually. When we reached the border, it seemed like one problem after another kept popping up. As soon as we would figure out a solution to one, something else would happen to set us back again. There was an issue with the medications we were bringing with us, one of the team members didn't have the correct paperwork, and on and on. We were getting really discouraged! I remember one of our translators stood in front of us and said, "We are a group of Christians traveling to Mexico to share the Gospel and serve a community. The devil is not going to sit back and make this easy! Every time we hit a roadblock, I say we rise up against it with prayer!" And, that's just what we did! Whenever we encountered an obstacle, we prayed right through it. We said a lot of STAN prayers on that trip. Ultimately, people were helped, the church grew, and God was glorified!

Prayers in the moment remind you that God is in control of every aspect of your life.

God is the one person that you want involved in every single decision that you're making and every action that you're taking. Every situation that you're in, you want God to be right in the middle of it. And so prayers in the moment are extremely important. They are empowering. When you are faced with something hard, it is comforting and helpful to know that in that moment you can call out God in prayer: "This is going to be hard right now, and I need your help right now!" I encourage you to pray those prayers in the moment. I've told my children that when they're faced with something tough, the first thing they should do is to invite God into that problem. He's the one you want beside you above anyone and anything else! Prayers for STAN can be for all types of circumstances! For my children, it might be that they're about to take a test and they want to ask God for help focusing. It might be that we're driving down the street and all of a sudden, we're in a massive rainstorm and it's scary, and we want to ask God for protection. It might be that I need to have a difficult conversation with someone, and I want to ask God for help choosing the right words.

Those are all prayers in a moment, and they are important because they are faith building. Prayers in the moment remind you that God is in control of every aspect of your life. When you stop in the middle of life's craziness and remember that nothing is too big for God to handle and that His throne is always approachable, you allow His peace and His power to fill your heart and overflow into the world around you. These prayers can happen at any time, at any moment. I have received texts before saying, "I have this going on right now—" or "This is about to happen right now—would you stop and pray for me?" A thousand times, yes! What an honor! I've stopped in the middle of the fruits and veggies section at Publix and raised up a prayer for STAN. I've had friends pray with me in the middle of the day at school when I needed strength. Prayers "in the moment" are times when you need God's help now and if they aren't a part of your prayer life, I encourage you to begin praying them today.

Prayer Prompt

As your prayer prompt for today, I picked a verse found in Psalm 86. *"Give ear, O Lord, to my prayer, and attend to the voice of my supplications. In the day of my trouble I will call upon You, for You will answer me"* (Psalm 86:6-7). When you have trouble, whether it's a day of trouble, a week of trouble, a month of trouble, a year of trouble, or a moment of trouble, call on God first. You will have invited the most powerful, most influential, most helpful person that you could possibly ask into that situation from the beginning. Pray for God to grant you whatever it is that you need in difficult, frightening, or stressful—right then and there! God will answer your prayer and you will be able to get through it. Try that today! Take moments of trial to God in prayer and see what happens.

Prayer Journal

O Lord God, remember me, I pray! Strengthen me, I pray just this once, O God, that I may with one blow take vengeance on the Philistines for my two eyes.

JUDGES 16:28

1. Who was praying in this Scripture reference and what were the circumstances leading up to this moment?

2. What was the purpose of this prayer?

3. How did God answer?

4. Read Genesis 24:12-14. Who was praying here and what was the purpose of this prayer?

5. Would these two specific prayer requests have been offered as part of a daily prayer regimen? Why or why not?

6. What do we learn from these prayers that we can apply to our personal prayer lives?

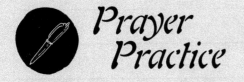 *Prayer Practice* Read the words found in Psalm 86:6-7. Remember that God listens to our prayers in our "day of trouble" and that He answers! As you are faced with situations throughout the day that are challenging, or as you run into difficult circumstances—however big or small they might seem— stop right then and pray. Immediately take those hard moments to God in prayer—ask for "strength to act now!" He is the one you want working with you and for you in those moments!

_____

_____

_____

_____

_____

_____

_____

I will extol you, O Lord, for You have lifted me up and have not let my foes rejoice over me. O Lord my God, I cried out to You, and You healed me. O Lord, You brought my soul up from the grave. You have kept me alive, that I should not go down to the pit.

Sing praise to the Lord, you saints of His, and give thanks at the remembrance of His holy name; for His anger is but for a moment, His favor is for life. Weeping may endure for a night, but joy comes in the morning.

Now in my prosperity I said, 'I shall never be moved.' Lord, by Your favor You have made my mountain stand strong. You hid your face, and I was troubled.

I cried out to you, O Lord, and to the Lord I made supplication. 'What profit is there in my blood when I go down to the pit? Will the dust praise you? Will it declare Your truth? Hear, O Lord, and have mercy on me. Lord, be my helper!'

You have turned for me my mourning into dancing; you have put off my sackcloth and clothed me with gladness, to the end that my glory may sing praise to You and not be silent. O Lord my God, I will give thanks to You forever.

PSALM 30

Prayer Three

PSALM 30

The Prayer

David, God's chosen king and the man with a God-like heart, is the one who humbly prayed the words of this psalm.

Previously...

What circumstances lead up to this prayer of David's? First, take a look in your Bible and see if there is a subtitle that appears underneath the book and chapter number that might give you an indication of what this psalm is about. In my King James Version, the subtitle reads "The Blessedness of Answered Prayer" and just below that it says, "A psalm. A song at the dedication of the house of David." Those words give a little clue as to what was happening here and what had just occurred. There are differing opinions when you read commentaries about this particular psalm. Some believe that this was a song or prayer that was being sung at the dedication of David's house, the place where David actually lived—a palace of some sort. Others believe that this prayer was more prophetic and referred to the Lord's house—the temple that was going to be built under the rule of David's son Solomon. Regardless of which view is taken, the content of the prayer is not changed and the message remains the same. It is my belief that David was speaking about the dedication of his personal house, and if we spend some time in the first few chapters of 2 Samuel, we will discover the events that led up to the building of David's palace.

Have you ever traveled a broken road that ultimately led to blessing?

The book of 2 Samuel begins with the announcement of the death of Saul and his son Jonathan. Their actual deaths are described at the close of 1 Samuel in chapter 31. Three days later, a messenger brought the news to David, and when David heard, he was completely distraught. Toward the end of the first chapter of 2 Samuel, we find that David lamented over the deaths of Saul and Jonathan, and he instructed that a song be taught to the children of Judah, entitled "The Song of the Bow." The words to that song are recorded in 2 Samuel 1:19-27. In the second chapter, David was anointed as king of Judah. It was God's intention to have him rule over all of Israel, but in the text, we find that after Saul's death, Abner, the commander of Saul's army, took Ish-bosheth, who was Saul's son, and made him king over Israel. With David ruling over Judah and Ish-bosheth ruling over Israel, division permeated the Israelite nation. As you work through the next few chapters, you will read about some horrendous murders that take place and a series of events that are quite rough, but that will eventually lead to the anointing of David over the entire nation.

By the time you reach chapter 5, David has been made king over all of Israel, and verse 11 says, "*Then Hiram, king of Tyre, sent messengers to David, and cedar trees, and carpenters and masons. And they built David a house.*" The following verse states that David knew the Lord had established him as king over Israel and that He had exalted His kingdom for the sake of His people Israel. And so, a place was built for David—a home--a palace, perhaps—something fit for a king. David recognized that it was the Lord who had established him as king, that it was the Lord's kingdom, and that the Israelite nation belonged to the Lord. He didn't feel as if any of that was his own. He knew that the credit and glory belonged to God.

The Purpose

The words of this prayer were spoken in order to give thanks, to give glory to God, to express gratitude over what the Lord had given to David. Remember, this was coming off of years of David running, hiding, and having his life threatened by Saul. Then the time came and the Lord placed him on the throne as ruler of His people, and David is grateful. Look at the first words of Psalm 30: "*I will extol you, O Lord.*" To "extol" is to give high praise or to lift up. David said that he would "give high praise" to the Lord because He lifted him up and had not let his enemies rejoice over him. David is thankful and he is expressing his thanksgiving to the Lord. Moving down into verse 2, there's another hint of something for which David is grateful: "*O Lord my God, I cried out to you and you healed me.*" It is possible that David had actually been healed from some type of physical illness; and if not physical, then he had certainly been in mental and emotional anguish concerning the things he had suffered in his spirit over the years. Could it be that it was David's broken heart that had received God's healing? Maybe God healed him in that way? It could be something like that, but either way, he is giving thanks to God. In verse 4 David says, "*Sing praise to the Lord, you saints of His, and give thanks at the remembrance of His holy name.*" The intention of David's prayer is found in these words: "sing praise" and "give thanks." Then, take a look at the very last line of this psalm. A beautiful promise was made by David. "*I will give thanks to You forever.*" David tells the Lord that his gratitude was going to be continual—never-ending—lasting forever. It is going to go on forever. What a lovely prayer of thanks!

Now, turn in your Bible to John 11. Let's shift our focus to another prayer while keeping in mind the concept of communicating our thanks to God. The account of Lazarus being raised from the dead is found here and in verses 41 and 42, we read the words of a prayer spoken by Jesus. You may remember this story. Jesus had been summoned by his friends Mary and Martha because their brother Lazarus was sick, and they knew that Jesus loved him. But, Jesus did not leave right away, in fact, He stayed two more days in the place where He was, and by the time He arrived, Lazarus was dead. Beginning in verse 38, the text says, "*Then Jesus, again groaning in himself, came to the tomb. It was a cave, and a stone lay against it. Jesus said, 'Take away the stone.' Martha, the sister of him who was dead, said to Him, 'Lord, by this time there is a stench, for he has been dead for four days.' And Jesus said to her, 'Did I not say to you that if you would believe, you would see the glory of God?' And they took away the stone from the place where the dead man was lying. And Jesus lifted up His eyes and said, 'Father, I thank You that You have heard Me. And I know that You always hear Me, but because of the people who are standing by I said this, that they may believe that You sent Me.' Now when He had said these things, He cried with a loud voice, 'Lazarus, come forth!' And he who had died came out bound hand and foot with grave clothes, and his face was wrapped with a cloth. And Jesus said to them, 'Loose him, and let him go.'*" I love the story of the raising of Lazarus for a lot of reasons. I love it because it shows us again the compassionate, kind, and caring side of Jesus that we see so much in the Gospels. He wept with those whom He loved. He knew that He was going to raise Lazarus and yet, He grieved with the people who were there. He grieved with them because He loved them and He felt their sorrow. It also must have pained Him to know that even though He was about to demonstrate His divine power to them through a miracle, they would still reject Him as the Son of God, their Messiah.

Notice the words of Jesus in verses 41 and 42: "*Father, I thank You that You have heard Me.*" Jesus, the Son of God, our Savior, the Messiah, the Christ is stopping to thank His Father. Why do you think He did that? He actually tells us why He did it in these words of His prayer: "*I know You hear Me, but I am saying this out loud so that these people around here will have no doubt that You are God and I am your Son and that You hear Me and I am here to do Your will."* Jesus offered that prayer of thanksgiving even before He spoke the words, *"Lazarus, come forth."* He knew that God would hear Him. He thanked God for what was about to happen and for the testimony that it was going to be in the presence of all those people. Jesus took time to say "thank you"—an important lesson for us today when it comes to the purpose and privilege of prayer.

And God Said...

Why are prayers of this nature important to bring to the throne of God? Why is thanksgiving something that we should make a part of our regular prayer lives? Turn in your Bible to 1 Thessalonians 5:18 and read what Paul told the church at Thessalonica about this subject. Beginning in verse 16, Paul wrote, *"Rejoice always, pray without ceasing; in everything give thanks, for this is the will of God in Christ Jesus for you."* It's important to be thankful and to express our thanks to God because it is His will for us. That's number one! We do it because it's God's desire and expectation for us. Another reason we want to express prayers of thanksgiving is because it helps to keep our hearts in a right relationship with God. It reflects our love and our respect for Him. It reminds us to continually recognize His goodness and mercy.

It's important to be thankful and express our thanks to God because it is His will for us.

When you've given something to somebody and really considered a gift that would be helpful to that person--something they could use and enjoy; isn't it wonderful to receive back from them a note or a word of thanks for the gift that you gave? It makes you feel appreciated! To say "thank you" is a wonderful way to recognize someone else's good deed. That is what prayers of thanksgiving do as we lift them up to our Heavenly Father. We acknowledge that He is the kind and loving gift-giver, and that He blesses us in countless ways every day. We guard against becoming self-centered and arrogant or thinking that we are deserving of all the good that God has showered down on us. When we take time to tell God "thank you," we are practicing humility and plainly saying, "I recognize what You've done for me, and I am grateful."

The Present

What can we learn from these types of prayers and what can we apply to our own personal prayer lives? I believe the lesson is this: Do not neglect to pay special attention to expressing thanksgiving in prayer. Make sure that it's something that you do regularly. Think about all of your blessings. Think about the things you have in your life that you would not want to go without. Think about those things that bring joy to your everyday life and remember that God is the source of all those good things (James 1:17). God fills our lives with things to bring us happiness, to take care of us, to offer us help, to sustain us, and to give us strength to get through trials and temptations, and He deserves our gratitude. We should cultivate the habit of thanking God in our prayers for the compassionate way He shows us His loving-kindness.

Years ago, when my daughter Evie was around four years old, she walked into the kitchen while I was cooking dinner. She took one look at what we were going to be eating that night and immediately decided she was not interested! She told me that she wanted something else to eat and I explained that she would be eating exactly what the rest of us would be eating. For the next 30 minutes or so, she continued to remind me that she did not like what we were having for dinner that night. When we all sat down to eat, we asked Evie if she would like to say the prayer. She folded her little hands and sweetly started, "Dear God, thank you for this food." As soon as the words came out of her mouth, she realized what she had just said, and quickly exclaimed with complete honesty, "Wait! I did **not** mean to say that!" Evie caught herself saying something in prayer that she did not intend to say at all. Sam and I had to do some teaching in that moment about gratitude, but she also inadvertently taught us a lesson on the importance of sincerity when speaking to God in prayer!

Prayer Prompt

For your prayer prompt, consider the words of Chronicles 16:34. "O give thanks to the Lord, for He is good; for His mercy endures forever." My challenge for you today is to say a prayer that focuses only on thanksgiving. It doesn't have to be (and shouldn't be) your only prayer today but do take time to focus your heart on a prayer of thanks, recognizing God and giving Him glory and honor for the things that He has given you. It would be a wonderful thing for us to get in the habit of doing every day! Expressing our gratitude to God should be something that we do regularly, willingly, and lovingly.

I will extol you, O Lord, for You have lifted me up and have not let my foes rejoice over me. O Lord my God, I cried out to You, and You healed me. O Lord, You brought my soul up from the grave. You have kept me alive, that I should not go down to the pit.

Sing praise to the Lord, you saints of His, and give thanks at the remembrance of His holy name; for His anger is but for a moment, His favor is for life. Weeping may endure for a night, but joy comes in the morning.

Now in my prosperity I said, 'I shall never be moved.' Lord, by Your favor You have made my mountain stand strong. You hid your face, and I was troubled.

I cried out to you, O Lord, and to the Lord I made supplication. 'What profit is there in my blood when I go down to the pit? Will the dust praise you? Will it declare Your truth? Hear, O Lord, and have mercy on me. Lord, be my helper!'

You have turned for me my mourning into dancing; you have put off my sackcloth and clothed me with gladness, to the end that my glory may sing praise to You and not be silent. O Lord my God, I will give thanks to You forever.

PSALM 30

1. Who was praying in this Scripture reference and does your Bible give any indication, in the subtitle of this psalm, of the circumstances leading up to this moment?

2. What was the purpose of this prayer?

3. What promise is made in the very last line of this prayer?

4. Read John 11:41-42. Who is praying and for what purpose?

5. Why are prayers of this nature important to bring to the throne of God?

6. What do we learn from these prayers that we can apply to our personal prayer lives?

Prayer Practice

Today when you pray, be sure to include a prayer dedicated to thanksgiving. God is the giver of good gifts. Thank Him for the blessings in your life: the prayers He has answered, the hope He has provided. Thank Him for Jesus. Thank Him for the Bible. Thank Him for the church. Thank Him, thank Him, and thank Him some more (1 Chronicles 16:34).

_____

_____

_____

_____

O Lord, great and awesome God, who keeps His covenant and mercy with those who love Him, and with those who keep His commandments, we have sinned and committed iniquity, we have done wickedly and rebelled, even by departing from Your precepts and Your judgments. Neither have we heeded Your servants the prophets, who spoke in Your name to our kings and our princes, to our fathers and all the people of the land....

...And now, O Lord our God, who brought Your people out of the land of Egypt with a mighty hand, and made Yourself a name, as it is this day—we have sinned, we have done wickedly! O Lord, according to all Your righteousness, I pray, let Your anger and Your fury be turned away from Your city Jerusalem, Your holy mountain; because for our sins, and for the iniquities of our fathers, Jerusalem and Your people are a reproach to all those around us.

Now therefore, our God, hear the prayer of Your servant, and his supplications, and for the Lord's sake cause Your face to shine on Your sanctuary, which is desolate. O my God, incline Your ear and hear; open Your eyes and see our desolations, and the city which is called by Your name; for we do not present our supplications before You because of our righteous deeds, but because of Your great mercies.

O Lord, hear! O Lord, forgive! O Lord, listen and act! Do not delay for Your own sake, my God, for Your city and Your people are called by Your name.

DANIEL 9:13-19

Prayer Four

DANIEL 9:13-19

The Prayer

This was a prayer of confession offered to God by Daniel the prophet on behalf of the Israelite nation. His words recalled the transgressions that had been committed by Israel against God and he asked for their forgiveness. Daniel pleaded for God to hear his prayer and to turn away His wrath.

Previously...

What happened in Israelites' history that led up to this point? In the book of Daniel, we find that the Israelite nation, specifically the kingdom of Judah, had been taken into Babylonian captivity. Daniel was a young man when he was taken to the city of Babylon and called on to serve in the royal court of King Nebuchadnezzar. The first six chapters are a recollection of history and tell the story about what was happening to Daniel during that time of captivity. He served the kings as an advisor, and at one point he was placed in command of the wise men of Babylon. He was a good, good man, to the extent that he was even recognized for his strength of character by the kings of Babylon, and then later by the king of Persia. Above all, we know that Daniel remained faithful to God throughout that entire time. He was a righteous man, a prayerful man, a man of integrity, and a man of conviction. He was a man who continually stood up for the Lord. In fact, I don't know that there are any stories that reflect anything negative about God's servant Daniel.

In what ways can you stand up for the Lord in a world that often rejects Him?

The last part of the book, from chapter 7 to the end, describes prophetic visions sent to Daniel by God. In the first six chapters, we see Daniel as the interpreter of visions, but in the last half of the book as the receiver of visions. The prophecies that Daniel received spoke about the kingdom of God that would be established and that would never, never fall. God revealed what would happen with the nations of the world and how they would crumble, but that there would be a kingdom coming that would not be destroyed. The entire book of Daniel is an amazing testimony to the wisdom and sovereignty of God and His glorious, eternal purpose.

The Purpose

In chapter 9 we come to this prayer spoken by Daniel. At the very beginning of the chapter, we learn that King Darius was ruling, as the Medes and the Persians had conquered Babylon ("the realm of the Chaldeans"); and Daniel referred to something that happened in the first year of Darius' reign. He had found something that revealed vital information to him. In verse 2, the Bible says, *"I, Daniel, understood by the books the number of the years specified by the word of the Lord through Jeremiah the prophet, that He would accomplish seventy years in the desolations of Jerusalem."* Daniel had discovered the 70-year prophecy of captivity in the writings of Jeremiah! Once Daniel received that information, he "set his face toward the Lord God" and began to pray. In other words, he turned his attention fully toward God. Then, he approached God with confession on behalf of the Israelite people and asked God for His forgiveness. He begged God in prayer for His anger and fury to be turned away from His city of Jerusalem.

It's important to recognize the physical state that Daniel was in when He came before God with his words of repentance. Notice in verse 3 how Daniel described the way in which he offered his prayer and supplications: *"...with fasting, sackcloth, and ashes."* This is a picture of mourning! It demonstrated subjection and humility before God. Daniel was in sorrow over the sins of the Israelite nation and his attitude reflected true sincerity as He pleaded with God for mercy

And God Said...

Did God answer this prayer? We **know** that He did! In fact, there had already been a number of prophecies made concerning how God was going to forgive His people and how there would be a return to Jerusalem. The Israelites would come out of captivity and return to their land. God **did** answer their prayer! He **did** forgive them and allow them to come back.

In Isaiah 65:24 God spoke these words to His prophet Isaiah: "*It shall come to pass, that before they call, I will answer; and while they are still speaking, I will hear.*" In keeping with that promise, the Bible says that while Daniel was "speaking, praying, and confessing" his sin and the sin of the Israelite nation, the angel Gabriel came to him in a vision with a message. What followed was one of the most telling Messianic prophecies in the Old Testament! Gabriel revealed to Daniel the purpose of Jesus Christ coming to earth and presented a precise timeline for His arrival and His death.

Daniel was described by Gabriel as being "greatly beloved" by God (Daniel 9:23). Certainly, God had looked down on Daniel and seen his faithfulness, his integrity, and his humility and chose to give him a glimpse into His sovereign will. Even as Daniel's prayer of confession was beginning, God sent Gabriel to deliver to him a most exceptional understanding of a most exceptional plan. A divine plan that would not only change the lives of the Israelites, but all of mankind, for eternity.

The Present

The assurance that we have today is that God still hears our prayers of confession and He offers us His forgiveness. We read these words in 1 John 1:8-9, "*If we say that we have no sin, we deceive ourselves, and the truth is not in us. If we confess our sins, He is faithful and just to forgive us our sins and to cleanse us from all unrighteousness.*" These verses tell us that we all sin, but if we come before God with a broken and contrite heart, and confess our sins to Him, He will forgive us and make us clean! That is a promise that we've been given. The ability to have our sins forgiven is a spiritual blessing for those who are in Christ. It's a comfort to know that when we fall into sin, we can always return to God. When the prodigal son came back home, the first words he spoke were, "Father, I have sinned." Our words should be the same to our Heavenly Father when we leave the path of sin and find our way back home.

However, prayers of confession are not always easy. It can be hard to call out sin in our own lives and it can be even harder to take ownership of our sin-struggles in the presence of the One who paid the price for them. It may be embarrassing, or it might make us feel ashamed, but it is a necessary step to take in order to be forgiven. Confession is also difficult, because it acknowledges a need to change, and change requires action! Once we have taken that first step, it becomes our responsibility to remove that sin, or the temptation, from our lives. That takes strength, perseverance, and the help and prayers of our Christian family (James 5:16).

Even if we find this type of prayer challenging, we can find guidance in Daniel's words of confession. Notice that first, he recognized God's goodness and power. As he began his prayer he said, "*O Lord, great and awesome God, who keeps His covenant and mercy with those who love Him, and with those who keep His commandments.*" Daniel referred to God's glorious divine nature all throughout his prayer, again and again identifying Him as righteous and merciful. Secondly, Daniel was specific in his admission of sin. He didn't use vague phrases like, "If we've fallen short…" or "We want to do better…." Instead, he made it clear that God's people had disobeyed and fallen into sin: "*We have sinned and committed iniquity, we have done wickedly and rebelled, even by departing from Your precepts and Your judgments…We have not obeyed the voice of the Lord our God, to walk in His laws, which He set before us by His servants the prophets…We have sinned, we have done wickedly!*" Daniel was honest and straightforward about the sins of the Israelites. Next, he knew that they deserved the consequences they had faced because of their sin and he expressed that to God in his prayer: "*O Lord to us belongs shame of face…all Israel has transgressed Your law, and has departed so as not to obey Your voice; therefore the curse and the oath written in the Law of Moses the servant of God have been poured out on us, because we have sinned against Him.*" Finally, Daniel appealed to God for forgiveness and restoration. He begged for God to hear his prayer and to act quickly in turning away His anger: "*I pray let your anger and Your fury be turned away…cause Your face to shine on Your sanctuary…O Lord, hear! O Lord, forgive! O Lord, listen and act!*"

The ability to have our sins forgiven is a spiritual blessing for those who are in Christ.

When we come before God with sins we need to confess, we should remember the heart of Daniel and how he prayed with a spirit of mourning, in humility and sorrow over the unfaithfulness of Israel. We can follow his example in prayer by recognizing God's power, by being specific in our admission of sin, understanding the consequences of sin, and asking for His forgiveness of our sin. Simon the sorcerer offered Peter and John money for the power to give the Holy Spirit to people by laying his hands on them. In Acts 8:22, Peter told Simon, "*Repent therefore of this your wickedness, and pray God if perhaps the thought of your heart may be forgiven you.*" God hears our prayers of confession and He forgives.

 *Prayer Prompt*

Daniel's prayer in Daniel 9 teaches us that we should not forget the importance of prayers of confession. We can't neglect to confess our sins to God and to ask for His forgiveness. He has promised to forgive us and even more, to not keep a record of our wrongs; but we must come to Him in repentance and lay our iniquities at His feet. We do this with a humble heart through prayer. Reflect on the words that David wrote in Psalm 32:5, *"I acknowledged my sin to You, and my iniquity I have not hidden. I said, 'I confess my transgressions to the Lord,' and You forgave the iniquity of my sin."* David, the man after God's own heart, was not a stranger to sin. He messed up. He fell short. He did things that were wrong. But he knew that if he acknowledged his mistakes and if he confessed those sins in sincerity and with the desire to live righteously, the Lord would forgive him. David lived his life with that confidence.

Today, I encourage you to pray a prayer of confession. What do you need to release from your heart? What do you need to turn over to God? What struggle in your life do you need to talk to Him about? Pray about it! Pray for forgiveness and pray for strength to keep fighting the good fight of faith. I would also suggest that as part of a prayer of confession that you ask God to help you to let go of guilt. Sometimes guilt can help us to reset our focus and nudge us back in the right direction; but if we let guilt settle inside our hearts, it will begin to create a wedge between us and our relationship with God. We can't give guilt a place to camp out because its quiet whisper will soon become a persistent shout of "You're No Good!" We need to talk to God about it, and we need to kick guilt out, and we need to know that we can start afresh. When we confess our sins, He is faithful and He's willing to forgive us of those things.

O Lord, great and awesome God, who keeps His covenant and mercy with those who love Him, and with those who keep His commandments, we have sinned and committed iniquity, we have done wickedly and rebelled, even by departing from Your precepts and Your judgments. Neither have we heeded Your servants the prophets, who spoke in Your name to our kings and our princes, to our fathers and all the people of the land....

...And now, O Lord our God, who brought Your people out of the land of Egypt with a mighty hand, and made Yourself a name, as it is this day--we have sinned, we have done wickedly! O Lord, according to all Your righteousness, I pray, let Your anger and Your fury be turned away from Your city Jerusalem, Your holy mountain; because for our sins, and for the iniquities of our fathers, Jerusalem and Your people are a reproach to all those around us.

Now therefore, our God, hear the prayer of Your servant, and his supplications, and for the Lord's sake cause Your face to shine on Your sanctuary, which is desolate. O my God, incline Your ear and hear; open Your eyes and see our desolations, and the city which is called by Your name; for we do not present our supplications before You because of our righteous deeds, but because of Your great mercies.

O Lord, hear! O Lord, forgive! O Lord, listen and act! Do not delay for Your own sake, my God, for Your city and Your people are called by Your name.

DANIEL 9:13-19

1. Who was praying in this Scripture reference and what were the circumstances leading up to this moment?

2. What was the purpose of this prayer?

3. In what physical state did the person offering the prayer approach God? (v. 3)

4. Did God answer this prayer?

5. What assurance do we have from God in 1 John 1:9?

6. What do we learn from this prayer that we can apply to our personal prayer lives?

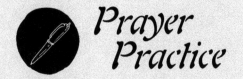

Prayer Practice

Today, I challenge you to spend time in a prayer of confession. Talk to God about specific sins you have committed, or temptations that you continually struggle with, or the good things that you know you should do but sometimes don't. Place these confessions at His feet and ask for Him to forgive you, to strengthen you, and to help you fight against the weakness of the flesh and the schemes of the devil. He will, because He loves you!! God doesn't expect perfection...He wants a faithful heart that longs to serve Him!

_____

_____

_____

_____

_____

_____

_____

_____

_____

_____

_____

_____

_____

_____

_____

_____

_____

_____
_____
_____
_____
_____
_____
_____
_____
_____
_____
_____
_____
_____
_____
_____
_____
_____
_____
_____
_____
_____

For this reason I bow my knees to the Father of our Lord Jesus Christ, from whom the whole family in heaven and earth is named, that He would grant you, according to the riches of His glory, to be strengthened with might through His Spirit in the inner man, that Christ may dwell in your hearts through faith; that you, being rooted and grounded in love, may be able to comprehend with all the saints what is the width and length and depth and height—to know the love of Christ which passes knowledge; that you may be filled with all the fullness of God.

Now to Him who is able to do exceedingly abundantly above all that we ask or think, according to the power that works in us, to Him be glory in the church by Jesus Christ to all generations, forever and ever. Amen.

EPHESIANS 3:14-21

Prayer Five

EPHESIANS 3:14-21

The Prayer

This section of Scripture is found in the book of Ephesians, which was written as a letter from the apostle Paul to the church in Ephesus. The Ephesian church was made up of Gentile Christians and Paul's message to them was you are a part of the body of Christ! He wanted them to know that being *in Christ* meant that they were no longer separate. Jesus had come and torn down the middle wall of separation, bringing Jews and Gentiles together as one, and establishing peace. Paul, by inspiration, told the Ephesians that Jesus had reconciled both Jews and Gentiles to God in one body through the cross. That message was woven throughout the letter. Paul also wanted them to know their identity in Christ—what that truly meant and what comes with that relationship. He addressed that in the first several chapters of the letter; and in the last few chapters he explained how they should live based on that identity. And right there wedged between the "who you are" and "how you should live" is this wonderful prayer.

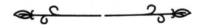

Previously…

Let's just start right at the beginning of the prayer, which is in verse 14 of Ephesians chapter 3. Paul's first words were, "*For this reason I bow my knees….*" To fully grasp the meaning of Paul's prayer, you have to start by asking the question, "For *what* reason?" What was the reason he bowed his knees to pray this particular prayer? To find the reason, you have to go back and read what was written before verse 14! Just like any verse that you look at in the Bible, it is so important that you consider context. Don't pull out one verse, or set of verses, and try to make them stand alone without understanding what was being said around them. When you're trying to break down and really study what a Scripture is saying, look at what comes before it and what comes after it. So, to understand the reason mentioned in verse 14, we have to go back. The goal is to go back until you reach the beginning of a complete thought. In this case, we are looking for the beginning of Paul's reason for his prayer in Ephesians 3:14-21. As you work backwards, keep in mind that if a verse begins with a transition word, or connecting word, you have to continue to go back. As you move back through chapter 3, you will reach the beginning of the chapter which also begins with the words, "*For this reason…*" And you have to keep going back! Eventually, you'll get to chapter 2 verse 19, which begins with the phrase, "*Now, therefore….*" We'll stop there and see what Paul was writing about that will give us an indication of the reason for his prayer. However, because the verse begins with the word "Now," it is also linked to what was written previously. I'm going to suggest that any letter that you read, to gain a full understanding of its contents and to keep all of the verses of that letter in context, you must read the entire letter. I believe that to be true of this epistle to the Ephesians.

Why is it important to consider context when you are studying Scripture?

In chapter 2:19, Paul wrote these inspired words, "*Now, therefore you are no longer strangers and foreigners, but fellow citizens with the saints and members of the household of God.*" Paul was saying to those Gentile Christians: This is who you are. You're members of the household of God. That's the church! Paul was talking about the church. You are no longer strangers and foreigners; you're part of God's family. "*…Having been built on the foundation of the apostles and prophets, Jesus Christ Himself being the chief cornerstone, in whom the whole building, being fitted together, grows into a holy temple in the Lord, in whom you also are being built together for a dwelling place of God in the Spirit.*" Paul said to the readers of his letter, "You are the church." Then as chapter 3 opens, he said, "For this reason…" and he continued to write first about the fact that Gentiles had become fellow heirs of the promise through the Gospel and how that had been the "mystery of Christ" throughout the ages; and then in verse 11, about the "eternal purpose of God." That purpose is presented in verse 10, which reads, "*To the intent that now the manifold wisdom of God might be made known by the church to the principalities and powers in the heavenly places, according to the eternal purpose which He accomplished in Christ Jesus our Lord.*"

Here is what Paul was telling these Gentiles Christians in Ephesus: First, you are the church. And second, you have a job. You are to show the world—it's your **responsibility** to show the world—the manifold wisdom of God that He achieved through Jesus Christ. That was God's eternal purpose! To send His Son, Jesus Christ, to offer up this plan of salvation for mankind so that **anyone** who believes it and follows it might be able to go home and be with Him for eternity. As the church, the Christians in Ephesus were supposed to show that to the world. That was their responsibility. So Paul was saying, because you're the church and because you are to show and communicate to the world the many beautiful and various ways that God's wisdom is demonstrated through Jesus Christ coming and dying on the cross for the salvation of mankind, **for this reason**, I bow my knees. Paul prayed on behalf of members of Christ's body, the church, and the crucial task they have been entrusted with—telling the world about what Jesus Christ accomplished through His death on the cross.

The Purpose

Paul's prayer was offered on the behalf of others. He doesn't ask for anything personally; he is praying for Christians and he is praying for their strength. That's where it all begins in this prayer: with strength. There's a reason why he started there for these fellow Christians. Paul's first specific request in this prayer can be found in verse 16. He prayed for them *"to be strengthened with might through His Spirit in the inner man."* This referred to the Spirit of God and the "inner man" was speaking about their spiritual selves. His prayer was for God, by the means of His Spirit, to strengthen their spirits. That was what Paul prayed for first, and his prayer advanced from that request, to the next request, and so on. In that way, Paul's prayer was a prayer of progression.

Notice how the prayer builds from beginning to end. Paul prayed for the spirits of the Christians to be strengthened by God's Spirit **so that** Christ might dwell in their hearts through faith. With a strong inner man, Christ could be settled in their hearts and live there through their faith **so that** they might be rooted and grounded in love and able to understand the love of Christ that surpasses knowledge **so that** they might be filled with the fullness of God. What began as Paul's prayer for strength would eventually lead to the ability to be partakers in the very nature of God. That is so powerful! But Paul's prayer does not end there! After Paul prayed for the Christians to be filled with the fullness of God, he had come to the end of his prayer and began his closing with the word *now*. It's almost as if Paul was saying, "All of these things I have prayed for you, and once all of that happens, **now** wait and watch and see what God will accomplish in your life." Now, because you've strengthened your inner man by His Spirit, and because now Christ is settled and at home in your hearts, and because now you can understand the love of Christ that surpasses knowledge, and because now you have been filled with the fullness of God, **now** to Him who is able to do exceedingly and abundantly more than all you ask or think, according to that power that's working in you, now to Him be the glory in the church by Jesus Christ to all generations forever and ever. Now that you have gained these things beginning with the strengthening of your spirit through the Holy Spirit, watch and see what God's going to accomplish through you, because it's going to be so much more than you could ever ask Him or even imagine that He could do. That is the prayer that Paul prayed for the church. It was a prayer for the good of others, that they may be strengthened. That was the first step. If the inner man is strengthened by the Spirit of God, then this is going to happen, this is going to happen, this is going to happen, and then comes the end, where more than you could ever think or possibly imagine, will be accomplished by God through you. An amazing prayer.

And God Said...

Why should we pray on the behalf of others? We could probably brainstorm many reasons why we should pray for other people, but one of the most important reasons is because when you pray for other people it causes you to think beyond yourself. It helps you put your own needs, your own concerns, your own desires to the side and think about other people. It's unselfish and it teaches us compassion. It encourages us to care about other people. There's something that is so incredibly powerful in knowing that somebody else has lifted your name up to the throne of God. It's comforting and strengthening at the same time. One of the greatest things that we can do for someone experiencing troubles, or when someone has needs, is to say, "I'm going to pray for you"—and then really do it. To pray on behalf of another is a gift that we can give our friends and our family and even those we may not know very well. I think of James 5:16, that says, "*Confess your trespasses to one another and pray for one another, that you may be healed. The effective, fervent prayer of a righteous man avails much.*" The working prayer life of a righteous person will accomplish a great deal.

I remember years ago one time that we were over at my in-laws' house, and Sam's dad mentioned that he prays for his children and their spouses and his grandchildren. He told me that he speaks each of our names in prayer every night, and I remember thinking how comforting that was to know that maybe on days when I let life get in the way of my talking to God, someone was still bringing my name into His presence. I know I can say that about other people, as well. I know that my mom and dad are praying for me and my family, and the sisters in my prayer group are praying for me, too. There's nothing better that we can do for each other than to lift one another up in prayer.

Let me also encourage you to try praying for a friend while you are in her presence. If the time and place is appropriate, and you have a sister talking to you about a need or a struggle that she is facing, ask her if she would like to pray together right then! It's such a gift to have someone who will take your hand, walk with you into God's presence, and beg Him in prayer for you. I'll never forget one day when I was working at Vanderbilt and pregnant with Evie, I passed through the food court and ran into a co-worker who I hadn't seen in quite a while. She stopped and asked me how I was doing and I told her that all was well except for feeling a little anxious about my pregnancy after having experienced a miscarriage a couple of years earlier. She immediately reached out for me and pulled me in a bit closer to her and whispered the words of a prayer into my ear. All of these years later, I still recall the comfort and peace I felt in that moment.

Another reason to pray for others can be found in Ephesians 6. This is the familiar text where Paul wrote about the Christian's spiritual armor—the armor that we wear in order to defend ourselves from the evil forces that are all around us, fighting for our souls. The components of our armor are described by Paul in verses 14-17. Then, in verse 18, another important aspect of our battle readiness is mentioned. Paul wrote, "*Praying always, with all prayer and supplication in the Spirit, being watchful to this end, with all perseverance and supplication for all the saints.*" Remember, the word saints here refers to Christians, and so Paul instructed Christians to pray for each other as part of their battle plan. Prayer supplies strength, protection, courage, and boldness. It's actually an extension of our armor provided for us and secured upon us by our Christian brothers and sisters. We help each other fight the good fight of faith when we take each other's needs and requests to God in prayer.

> **We help each other fight the good fight of faith when we take each other's needs and requests to God in prayer.**

The Present

Don't forget that this prayer of Paul's is as meaningful and applicable today as it was when it was written nearly 2000 years ago. Those prayerful words spoken for the Gentile Christians in Ephesus still speak for Christians today. Paul prayed for the strength of those who were a part of the church, and the same prayer rises from the pages of the Bible carrying as much power and as much promise as it did when Paul lifted the words to Heaven from bended knee.

One valuable lesson we learn from Paul's prayer in Ephesians 3:14-21 is the importance of praying for others. This should be a regular part of our prayer life—something that we do continually. Many times we might tell someone, "I'll be praying for you," and we must be careful that if we say we're going to do it that we follow through and take those prayers to God. Let me also encourage you to pray **with** others, right in their presence and right in the moment that it's needed or that they are asking. Maybe they're just talking to you about something they're struggling with, if you feel comfortable, stop them and offer to pray right then. It's uplifting. It's calming. It is comforting. It's a wonderful thing. Whether you pray with someone in person or in your own personal prayer time...just make it a habit to pray for others. You will be blessed as well.

Prayer Prompt

For your prayer prompt today, think about these words found in 1 Timothy 2:1, "Therefore I exhort first of all that supplications, prayers, intercessions, and giving of thanks be made for all men." The Greek word translated to "men" in that verse is more accurately translated "mankind" and is defined as both men and women. The word exhort means "to encourage" and supplications means "a pleading, or earnestly asking, for something." Prayers refers to our conversations with God or talking to God; and intercessions are when you step in to do something for somebody else. Here, in Scripture, we are encouraged to make supplications, prayers, and intercessions for all of mankind. Today, in your prayer time, pray at least one prayer that is completely for others. It may be that you have somebody in particular on your mind, someone who you want to pray specifically for or who has asked you to remember them in prayer—or maybe there are several people on your heart. Pick one or more people and pray for them exclusively in a prayer that you take to God.

Sometimes, if you're not able to think of the right words that you want to say, a helpful prayer exercise is to look up prayers of the Bible and pray the words of those prayers for someone else. For example, read Colossians 1:9-11. This is another one of Paul's prayers, included in his letter to the Christians at Colossae. It's a powerful prayer for spiritual transformation and growth. Try placing somebody else's name in it and pray for him using the words inspired by the Holy Spirit. Let me show you what that would look like using my husband's name. "Dear Father in Heaven, I ask that Sam may be filled with the knowledge of Your will, in all wisdom and spiritual understanding, that he may walk worthy and fully pleasing to You, being fruitful in every good work, and increasing in the knowledge of You; strengthened with all might according to Your glorious power, for all patience and longsuffering, with joy." Isn't that beautiful? It's a wonderful way to pray for others when you have a difficult time finding the right words. I encourage you to give it a try sometime!

For this reason I bow my knees to the Father of our Lord Jesus Christ, from whom the whole family in heaven and earth is named, that He would grant you, according to the riches of His glory, to be strengthened with might through His Spirit in the inner man, that Christ may dwell in your hearts through faith; that you, being rooted and grounded in love, may be able to comprehend with all the saints what is the width and length and depth and height--to know the love of Christ which passes knowledge; that you may be filled with all the fullness of God.

Now to him who is able to do exceedingly abundantly above all that we ask or think, according to the power that works in us, to Him be glory in the church by Jesus Christ to all generations, forever and ever. Amen.

EPHESIANS 3:14-21

1. Who was praying in this Scripture reference and what were the circumstances leading up to this moment?

2. What was the purpose of this prayer?

3. What were some of the specific requests that were made in this prayer?

4. Why should we pray on the behalf of others?

5. What does James 5:16 teach us about prayer?

6. **What do we learn from this prayer that we can apply to our personal prayer lives?**

Prayer Practice

Take some time today to lift up a prayer that is completely devoted to the needs and concerns of others. Maybe there is someone specific you have in mind? A family member? A friend? A person in a leadership position? Someone who has asked for the prayers of others? If you have a hard time thinking of the right words, try placing his or her name into the prayer described by Paul in Colossians 1:9-11 ("I pray that _____ may be filled with the knowledge of Your Will in all wisdom and spiritual understanding...)—it's so beautiful.

_____

_____

_____

_____

_____

_____

_____

My soul magnifies the Lord, and my spirit has rejoiced in God my Savior. For He has regarded the lowly state of His maidservant; for behold, henceforth all generations will call me blessed. For He who is mighty has done great things for me, and holy is His name. And His mercy is on those who fear Him from generation to generation. He has shown strength with His arm; He has scattered the proud in the imagination of their hearts. He has put down the mighty from their thrones, and exalted the lowly. He has filled the hungry with good things, and the rich He has sent away empty. He has helped His servant Israel, in remembrance of His mercy, as He spoke to our fathers, to Abraham and to his seed forever.

LUKE 1:46-55

LUKE 1:46-55

The Prayer

This is the beautiful prayer of Mary, the mother of Jesus.

Previously...

What was happening in Mary's life that led her to speak these words to God in prayer? If we go back to the beginning of the gospel of Luke we find some wonderful things were happening. First we have the announcement of the future birth of John the Baptist to Zacharias and his wife Elizabeth. We'll talk about that again in just a minute, but if you continue reading through chapter 1, in verse 26 we meet Mary. "*In the sixth month the angel Gabriel was sent by God to a city of Galilee named Nazareth, to a virgin betrothed to a man whose name was Joseph, of the house of David. And the virgin's name was Mary.*" So, here we have Mary being visited by the angel Gabriel. She was betrothed, which means that she was engaged, to a man named Joseph. It is also revealed here that she lived in Nazareth and that she was a virgin. The angel Gabriel had an extraordinary message for Mary. He told her, *"You are blessed among women, the Lord has favored you, He is with you."* Imagine this scene! Mary must have been terrified! The Bible doesn't give us the age of Mary, but secular history reveals her to be a young woman, likely in her teenage years. Here was a young woman confronted by an angel with an important message to convey. We know that she's scared because the angel specifically told her to not be afraid.

What are some things God has promised you that are worthy of praise?

In verse 31, we find the promise. Gabriel said, *"And behold, you will conceive in your womb and bring forth a son, and you shall call His name Jesus. He will be great, and will be called the Son of the highest; and the Lord God will give Him the throne of His father David. And He will reign over the house of Jacob forever, and of His kingdom there will be no end."* The prophecy is that Mary was going to have a child, and not just any child—she was going to give birth to the Son of God! The angel went on to tell her that the child's name was going to be Jesus, and that He would reign over a kingdom that would have no end. It startled Mary. She asked, *"How is this even possible? I have not known a man."* She had not been in a physical relationship with Joseph and wondered how it could be possible that she would have a child. The angel explained that it would be accomplished through the power of the Holy Spirit. And that was exactly what happened. The Holy Spirit allowed for Jesus to be conceived in the womb of Mary. It was an amazing and unprecedented miracle of the Holy Spirit!

As the chapter continues, Mary went to see her cousin Elizabeth who was mentioned earlier in the first chapter to Luke. Elizabeth had been told that she was going to have a son and that his name would be John. She was further told that many were going to rejoice at his birth, and he would "make the way ready for the Lord." When Mary first came into the presence of Elizabeth, the child in Elizabeth's womb leapt with joy! Elizabeth declared to Mary, *"Blessed are you among women, and blessed is the fruit of your womb! But why is this granted to me, that the mother of my Lord should come to me? For indeed, as soon as the voice of your greeting sounded in my ears, the babe leaped in my womb for joy. Blessed is she who believed, for there will be a fulfillment of those things which were told her from the Lord."* It is at this point that we come to the prayer spoken to Mary.

The Purpose

What was Mary's goal in speaking this prayer? What was her intention? The answer is simply praise. She praised God for what she had been chosen for, what would be accomplished through her, and who her child was going to be. Mary did not make any personal requests. Her focus was strictly on offering praise to God.

It's helpful to understand the difference between prayer and praise. Prayer involves talking to God about our feelings and our needs. We make our requests to Him through prayer. Prayer also involves our words of gratitude as well as our confessions. We draw close to God in prayer and have fellowship with the Creator of our very souls. Praise has another focus. Praise is the expression of our love and adoration for God. It doesn't involve asking Him for anything. It's focusing on glorifying Almighty God because of who He is and His presence in our lives. It's recognizing and honoring God for the holy attributes that He possesses and not expecting anything in return.

Mary could have been prideful over the fact that she had been chosen to be the earthly mother of the Messiah. She could have elevated herself in that God-given role, but her prayer reveals something much different. Mary humbled herself in her praise to God! She rejoiced that God had been mindful of her and had blessed her. She proclaimed Him to be mighty, holy, merciful, and strong, while she referred to herself as His maidservant in a lowly state. Mary's words came from a reverent and submissive heart in a powerful expression of praise.

And God Said...

Here is a question we should ask ourselves: "Why should we offer this type of prayer to God?" The number one reason we should offer prayers of praise or express any kind of praise to God is because we're commanded to do it. Isaiah 43:21 says, "This people I have formed for Myself; they shall declare My praise." Those are the words of God. He created people to praise Him. Hebrews 13:15 says, "*Therefore by Him let us continually offer the sacrifice of praise to God that is the fruit of our lips, giving thanks to His name.*" Then Psalm 150:6 says, "*Let everything that has breath praise the Lord.*" Why should we offer this type of prayer to God? First, because we're commanded to praise Him.

Along with the command to praise God, we praise Him because He deserves our praise. We talked already about how praise involves giving honor to someone who is worthy. God is worthy! He is all-powerful, all-knowing, and always present. He is sovereign, holy, just, kind, good, faithful, merciful, gracious, and He is love. When we study God's Word, we come to know His character more and more. As we gain a greater understanding of His nature, our response is to praise Him. We will praise God because we can't help but praise Him! We can have an attitude of thankfulness, which is gratitude for what God has done for us, and that certainly influences the idea of praise; but even more specifically, praise is offered simply for who

When we offer praise to God, we remind ourselves that we are not in charge and we are not our own.

God is.

Praising God in prayer involves benefits for the one praying as well. When we offer praise to God, we remind ourselves that we are not in charge and that we are not our own. We belong to God as His creation. We are His children, and praising Him reminds us of that. Praising God also helps us to refocus. It helps us to prioritize. Sometimes we get so caught up in our lives that we forget what is most important. We forget the power of the God we serve, and we lose sight of our purpose for being here. The Bible tells us that our purpose is to give glory to God and to bring glory to His name. Offering praise reminds us of that. When we praise God, it reminds us of who He is and the fact that He is even mindful of us. That should help our love for Him to grow and grow. It helps us calm our anxieties and fears because we are reminded that the omnipotent God cares about us as we go through trials and difficult times. Praising God takes the emphasis off of us and places it on His greatness, His goodness, and His holiness. It draws our mind away from this world and turns it toward our spiritual ambition...to be like Him! Praising God helps us to remember that He is in control and that we have a reason for being here.

The Present

Do you find a prayer of this nature difficult to pray or easy? Do prayers of praise come naturally to you? The answer to those questions will be different for everybody. It's something personal to think about. If it's hard, why is it hard? If you find these prayers a bit challenging—maybe because it's hard to find the right words, let me give you some suggestions that might help you in this area of your prayer life.

Writing down the characteristics of God, or the promises of God, can inspire our prayers of praise.

First of all, remember that praise does not only have to be offered in words. Praise can be lifted up in song. If you think of a song of praise that captures the goodness, the power, or the love of God, it would be lovely to sing that song of praise for Him. Just you alone, from your mouth and your heart, sing a song of praise to God. Think of a song that is special to you that describes your feelings about your Heavenly Father and consider singing that song in direct praise to God.

Another thing we can do is think about the characteristics of God and write them down. These should be words that you feel describe God. Here are some words that come to my mind: merciful, Creator, love, truth, good, strong, patient, majestic, holy, kind, and worthy. You could write down many, many words that capture the personality of God! Once you have created a list of words, use those words in a prayer of praise. Speak them out loud in prayer. Bring those words to the throne of God as words of praise. "I praise You for Your majesty. I praise You because You are my Creator. You are merciful and You are kind. Start by choosing words and writing them down and then work those words into a prayer.

One day, I walked into my son's room and saw the most amazing thing written on His dry erase wall. He had written G-O-D in really big letters and drawn a circle around it. Then coming off the circle he had drawn arrows and at the end of each arrow he had written a promise of God that we read in the Bible. *He will never leave me. He will work things together for my good. He will help me. He will give me strength.* I asked Briggs about his drawing and he said that when things are hard, or when he is worried or afraid, the promises keep him focused on God's faithfulness and love. First, I cried because that's just the sweetest thing ever, but second, I told him that it was a wonderful way to be reminded of how we serve a good God who always takes care of us. "I praise You for Your constant presence in my life. I praise You for Your help and guidance." Writing down the characteristics of God, or the promises of God, can inspire our prayers of praise.

Next, you can think about your blessings and use them as a way to praise God for the good things you have in your life. Like the exercise described above, you can make a list of your blessings and then praise God for all of those things you've written down. You can also think about God's blessings that are found in nature. Go on a walk! Find a trail to explore or even wander around your neighborhood, and as you walk, praise God for what you see and what you hear. That's a wonderful way to praise God through nature. As you see the trees, hear the birds, feel the breeze, or breathe in the fresh air, thank Him for all the things your senses experience in nature. Praise Him!

You can also write a poem of praise. Sometimes it might be easier for people to sit down and write something down on paper that expresses the glory and the majesty of God. Write your feelings about God in a poem, and then read those words back in prayer to God. You could also read Scriptures. In the Psalms you can find lots of songs and poems of praise. You can read those psalms in praise to God.

As another option, you can praise God by talking to somebody about what He means to you. If not directly in person, maybe imagine that there is somebody standing beside you and you want to tell that person what God means to you. Imagine what you would say, jot a few of those things down, and then bring them to God in a prayer of praise.

Mary's prayer teaches us that praise should be a part of our relationship with God today. It's something that we ought to be mindful of and it deserves an important and consistent place in our prayer lives. We are here to glorify God and to bring praise to Him. Our praise recognizes God for who He is and what He deserves.

Prayer Prompt

Today, praise God in prayer. Psalm 113:3 says, "*From the rising of the sun to its going down, the Lord's name is to be praised.*" All day the Lord's name is to be praised—from the moment we get up out of bed in the morning until we climb between the covers at night! Today set aside time for specific praise to God and talk to Him about how grateful you are because of who He is and what He means to you. I encourage you to do that today, and then find a way to make it a part of your prayer life regularly.

When you have the opportunity, look up an acapella version of the song "Magnificat" which is a portion of Mary's prayer in musical form. I urge you, after going through this lesson, to take some time to listen to that today. As you listen, think about the words of praise spoken by Mary when she found out what a wonderful, beautiful gift she had been given as the woman who had been chosen to be the mother of the Messiah

.

Prayer Journal

My soul magnifies the Lord, and my spirit has rejoiced in God my Savior. For He has regarded the lowly state of His maidservant; for behold, henceforth all generations will call me blessed. For He who is mighty has done great things for me, and holy is His name. And His mercy is on those who fear Him from generation to generation. He has shown strength with His arm; He has scattered the proud in the imagination of their hearts. He has put down the mighty from their thrones, and exalted the lowly. He has filled the hungry with good things, and

the rich He has sent away empty. He has helped His servant Israel, in remem-
brance of His mercy, as He spoke to our fathers, to Abraham and to his seed
forever.

LUKE 1:46-55

1. Who was praying in this Scripture reference and what were the circumstances leading up to this moment?

2. What was the purpose of this prayer?

3. Is anything being asked or requested by the person offering this prayer?

4. Why should we offer this type of prayer to God?

5. Do you find a prayer of this nature difficult to pray or easy? Why?

6. What do we learn from this prayer that we can apply to our personal prayer lives?

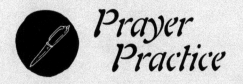

Prayer Practice

Your challenge today is to praise God. Try one of the suggestions that we talked about under question #5. In whatever form or method you choose, spend some time giving God the recognition He deserves, praising Him for who He is. Reflect on the words found in Psalm 113:3, "From the rising of the sun, to its going down, the Lord's name is to be praised!"

_____

_____

_____

_____

_____

_____

_____

_____

_____

_____

_____

_____

_____

_____

_____

_____

_____

_____

O Lord God of our fathers, are You not God in heaven, and do You not rule over all the kingdoms of the nations, and in Your hand is there not power and might, so that no one is able to withstand You? Are You not our God, who drove out the inhabitants of this land before Your people Israel, and gave it to the descendants of Abraham Your friend forever? And they dwell in it, and have built You a sanctuary in it for Your name, saying, if disaster comes upon us—sword, judgment, pestilence, or famine—we will stand before this temple and in Your presence (for Your name is in this temple), and cry out to You in our affliction, and You will hear and save. And now, here are the people of Ammon, Moab, and Mount Seir—whom You would not let Israel invade when they came out of the land of Egypt, but they turned from them and did not destroy them—here they are, rewarding us by coming to throw us out of Your possession which You have given us to inherit. O our God, will You not judge them? For we have no power against this great multitude that is coming against us; nor do we know what to do, but our eyes are upon You.

2 CHRONICLES 20:6-12

2 CHRONICLES 20:6-12

The Prayer

This was the prayer of one of the kings of Judah, a man by the name of Jehoshaphat.

Previously...

Who was this king Jehoshaphat? First, he ruled over the southern kingdom of Judah. At that time in Israelite history, the kingdom was divided into two kingdoms: the northern kingdom of Israel and the southern kingdom of Judah. In 2 Chronicles 17 we find that Jehoshaphat began his reign as king of Judah following the death of his father Asa. Also, we know that he was a good king (although he didn't always make the right choices, as we'll see later). In verses 3 through 6 of chapter 17, it says, "*Now the Lord was with Jehoshaphat, because he walked in the former ways of his father David; he did not seek the Baals, but sought the God of his father, and walked in His commandments and not according to the acts of Israel. Therefore the Lord established the kingdom in his hand; and all Judah gave presents to Jehoshaphat, and he had riches and honor in abundance. And his heart took delight in the ways of the Lord; moreover he removed the high places and wooden images from Judah."*

Jehoshaphat tried to do the right thing. He was faithful. He did not promote idolatry in his kingdom—the Bible says that he took away those wooden images and did not worship the Baals. He followed after the commandments of God and walked in the ways of his father David. However, in chapter 18 we read that he aligned himself with King Ahab, the ruler over the kingdom of Israel at that time. You might recognize the name Ahab! This is the same Ahab who was married to the evil queen Jezebel. Ahab was not a good king and did not follow in the ways of the Lord. There was a connection that Jehoshaphat had with Ahab through marriage and as a result, Jehoshaphat "allied himself with Ahab" (2 Chronicles 18:1). That relationship placed Jehoshaphat in a bad situation. It says in chapter 19 that the wrath of the Lord was upon him because of his alliance with Ahab. After going into battle with King Ahab against Ramoth Gilead despite the warning given through God's prophet Micaiah, another prophet Jehu confronted Jehoshaphat and said, "*Should you help the wicked and love those who hate the Lord? Therefore the wrath of the Lord is upon you*" (2 Chronicles 19:2). God was not pleased with Jehoshaphat, but if you continue to read through verse 3, Jehu went on to say, "*Nevertheless good things are found in you, Jehoshaphat, in that you have removed the wooden images from the land and have prepared your heart to seek God.*" Having heard those words from Jehu, Jehoshaphat initiated some reforms within his kingdom in order to bring the people back to God. He set up judges throughout the cities and instructed them to judge righteously for God. In Jerusalem, he also appointed some of the Levites, priests, and chief fathers of Israel as judges; and commanded them with these words: "*Thus you shall act in the fear of the Lord, faithfully and with a loyal heart.*" I love the final statement of Jehoshaphat recorded in chapter 19, "*Behave courageously, and the Lord will be with the good.*"

Have you ever been afraid to face someone or something and had to step out in courage?

Beginning in the next chapter, it's recorded that some of the people of Moab and Ammon along with some others had come together to fight against Jehoshaphat. In fact, they are described in verse 2 as a "great multitude." Jehoshaphat was afraid, but despite his fear, he "*set himself to seek the Lord*" (2 Chronicles 20:3). Jehoshaphat knew where to go. He was scared, but he knew where to turn. He knew his source of help. Jehoshaphat prayed. In verse 5, he stood in the house of the Lord before his people and spoke the words of the prayer we read in verses 6-12.

The Purpose

Look specifically again at the last couple of lines in verse 12. Jehoshaphat said to God, "*Nor do we know what to do; but our eyes are upon You.*" Here was Jehoshaphat in a situation that was hard, even terrifying, with the realization that he and his men were powerless against the large number of soldiers marching toward them in battle. He prayed, "*We have no power against this great multitude that is coming against us, nor do we know what to do, but our eyes are upon You.*" I love this about King Jehoshaphat, because it is so real, so relatable. It's such an incredible glimpse at his humanity. "I don't know what to do," he says, "but, I trust You, God." Jehoshaphat knew he needed help! He knew he needed power that he did not have! He also knew where to go to get both.

Have you ever prayed anything like that? Or, let me ask you this: Have you ever been in a situation where you really did not know what to do? Maybe it was a decision that you had to make—a choice—and it wasn't clear which was the bad choice, and which was the good choice. Maybe you have faced a challenge or a trial, and you didn't know the best way to handle it. Have you ever been in that situation where you just did not know what to do? This prayer of Jehoshaphat tells us exactly what you should do: You take it to God. Set down all of your uncertainty at the feet of your Father and say, "I don't know what to do, but I'm looking to You, I trust you, and I need Your help."

And God Said...

How did God respond to Jehoshaphat's prayer? We find His answer in verses 15 through 17. "*Listen, all you of Judah and you inhabitants of Jerusalem, and you, King Jehoshaphat! Thus says the Lord to you: Do not be afraid nor dismayed because of this great multitude, for the battle is not yours, but God's. Tomorrow go down against them. They will surely come up by the Ascent of Ziz, and you will find them at the end of the brook before the Wilderness of Jeruel. You will not need to fight in this battle. Position yourselves, stand still and see the salvation of the Lord, who is with you, O Judah and Jerusalem! Do not fear or be dismayed; tomorrow go out against them, for the Lord is with you.*" God's response to Jehoshaphat was: This battle is not yours—it's God's. Stand still, get into position, and see the salvation of the Lord who is with you. Don't be afraid. Go out tomorrow and know that the Lord is with you. I love how God said, "This battle belongs to Me." That is such a strengthening and encouraging response that God gave to Jehoshaphat. Notice, though, that God did not say "Stand still and do nothing." He said, "Tomorrow, **go out**, because I will be with you and you are going to see the salvation of the Lord." God assured Jehoshaphat that if he would go, God would be with him and would fight for him. I can only imagine how Jehoshaphat must have felt when he heard those words! I wonder if relief flooded over him? I wonder if he thought, "OK, I can do this, because God is going to help me."

It's interesting to compare God's response to Jehoshaphat and His response to Joshua in the battle of Jericho or His response to Gideon in the battle against the Midianites. The story of the battle of Jericho is found in Joshua 6 and we read about the story of Gideon and the battle against the Midianites in Judges 7. The answer God gave Jehoshaphat is quite different from the instruction He gave to Joshua and the strategy that He used through Gideon. The battles against Jericho and the Midianites were methodically carried out. In those situations there was a clear battle plan, and that was not the same case as seen in 2 Chronicles. With Jehoshaphat, there was no certain plan of attack, no battle blueprint. God's expectation of Jehoshaphat was to trust Him. He said, "This battle is Mine. I'm going to fight with you. Wait and see the salvation of the Lord." I am sure that Jehoshaphat must have had a hundred questions about that! There had to have been some thought over exactly how God would save them, but God's assurance to Jehoshaphat was, "You will be victorious. Trust Me." In all three of those battles, God was present. God promised victory, but the way in which that was accomplished was different in each circumstance. They all required trust. They all demanded a substantial amount of faith that God was going to be there fighting with them and for them.

The Present

What do we learn from this prayer that we can apply to our personal prayer lives? Most importantly, we learn that the very first thing we should do, especially when we don't know what to do, is take our difficult situations to God in prayer. We gather up our adversities, lay them at His feet, and say, "Father, I don't know what to do." Understand that this is a little different than not knowing what to say or not knowing how to express what you want to say. We have a promise in Romans 8 about how the Holy Spirit helps us in those times.

When you don't know what to do in any situation, the first thing to do is pray.

When we can't express what is in our hearts because we can't find the words, or because we don't know what to pray, Romans 8:26-27 says, "*Likewise the Spirit also helps in our weaknesses. For we do not know what we should pray for as we ought, but the Spirit Himself makes intercession for us with groanings which cannot be uttered. Now He who searches the hearts knows what the mind of the Spirit is, because He makes intercession for the saints according to the will of God.*" The Holy Spirit makes petitions on our behalf. He intervenes for us in our weaknesses. In Jehoshaphat's case, he had the words and knew what he wanted to ask, but he had no idea what to do. The lesson for us in those situations is to take your troubles, your anxieties, and your doubts to God. Involve Him first, and in all honesty and with all humility, pray the words, "I don't know what to do, but I trust You, and I need Your help. I need Your guidance. I want You to be with me in this battle."

There was one summer at Bible camp when I served as a counselor and all three of my kids were there as campers. One particular night, either the first or second night we were there, a little girl in my daughter Kate's cabin wanted to go home. She was having a hard time being away from home and she wanted to leave. It really upset Kate because she wanted her friend to stay and thought that if she would stay, she would realize how fun Bible camp is and she would have a great time. Kate came to find me in my cabin late that night. After she filled me in on everything that was going on she said, "I don't know what to do, Mom. I've prayed with her and asked for God's help, but I just don't know what else I should do." I remember looking at my then fourth-grade daughter who had just prayed with her friend, and telling her, "You have already done the most important thing that you could do. You took your problem to God, and you got Him involved at the very beginning. You may not know what to do, but you did the right thing by taking it to God in prayer." That's what we learn from Jehoshaphat. When you don't know what to do in any situation, the first thing to do is to pray.

We have to recognize that we are blessed today to have a divinely issued weapon to use in the spiritual battles we face in this world. While Jehoshaphat heard the words of God spoken through prophets, we also have God's words, found on the pages of the Bible, the sword of the Spirit. The Bible contains action plans! On its pages we discover battle strategy! We can know how to make good judgments when we're faced with challenges or temptations. We can hear the words of God advising us and giving us direction. We can go to His Word and learn how to grow stronger spiritually so that we are better prepared to handle trials that come our way and can make decisions based on truth. God still fights with us and for us, but it is also our responsibility to be well-trained soldiers, ready to "go out tomorrow" and face the enemy.

Prayer Prompt

For your prayer prompt today, listen first to the words of David found in Psalm 25:4-5. "*Show me Your ways, O Lord; teach me Your paths. Lead me in Your truth and teach me, for You are the God of my salvation; on You I wait all the day.*" It is in God's truth, His Word, that we find His ways and seek His paths. Read and study the Bible. Also, go to God in prayer in your times of uncertainty and fear and ask for His help. If there is something you're facing in your life right now and you really don't know what to do, or if you're not sure about a choice that you need to make, pray about it right now. Pray these words to God: "I'm looking to You. I don't know what to do. I'm not sure what option to take. I'm not certain about how to handle this situation. I'm asking for Your guidance and I'm in need of Your help." God will fight right beside you in your battle. Pray this prayer today—if not for yourself, pray on behalf of someone else who might be struggling through a difficult time. Remember that God is the God of your salvation; wait on Him and you will be blessed.

O Lord God of our fathers, are You not God in heaven, and do You not rule over all the kingdoms of the nations, and in Your hand is there not power and might, so that no one is able to withstand You? Are You not our God, who drove out the inhabitants of this land before Your people Israel, and gave it to the descendants of Abraham Your friend forever? And they dwell in it, and have built You a sanctuary in it for Your name, saying, if disaster comes upon us--sword, judgment, pestilence, or famine--we will stand before this temple and in Your presence (for Your name is in this temple), and cry out to You in our affliction, and You will hear and save. And now, here are the people of Ammon, Moab, and Mount Seir--whom You would not let Israel invade when they came out of the land of Egypt, but they turned from them and did not destroy them--here they are, rewarding us by coming to throw us out of Your possession which You have given us to inherit. O our God, will You not judge them? For we have no power against this great multitude that is coming against us; nor do we know what to do, but our eyes are upon You."

2 CHRONICLES 20:6-12

1. Who was praying in this Scripture reference and what were the circumstances leading up to this moment?

2. What was the purpose of this prayer?

3. Specifically looking at the last couple lines of verse 12, what was stated by the one offering the prayer?

4. What was God's response? (vs. 15-17)?

5. How does this differ from God's response to Joshua and the battle of Jericho or Gideon and the battle against the Midianites?

6. What do we learn from this prayer that we can apply to our personal prayer lives?

Prayer Practice

Is there a situation you've had on your heart that you're not sure how to handle? Is there a decision that you need to make and you're not clear about the right choice? Is there an enemy you're facing that you don't know how to defeat? Today, take it to God, lay it at His feet, and in the words of Jehoshaphat pray, "I don't know what to do, but my eyes are on You." Stand still and do not be afraid. Know that God is always with you and ask Him to help you fight your battles.

_____

_____

_____

Lord, You are God, who made heaven and earth and the sea, and all that is in them, who by the mouth of Your servant David have said, 'Why did the nations rage, and the people plot vain things? The kings of the earth took their stand, and the rulers were gathered together against the Lord and against His Christ.' For truly against Your holy Servant Jesus, whom You anointed, both Herod and Pontius Pilate, with the Gentiles and the people of Israel, were gathered together to do whatever Your hand and Your purpose determined before to be done. Now, Lord, look on their threats, and grant to Your servants that with all boldness they may speak Your word, by stretching out Your hand to heal, and that signs and wonders may be done through the name of Your holy Servant Jesus.

ACTS 4:24-30

Prayer Eight

ACTS 4:24-30

The Prayer

Who spoke the words of this prayer? Remember, that sometimes you have to look back through the text to find out who is speaking or what is being discussed in a given verse. We want to be careful to look at everything in context in the Bible. That's what we have to do here to find out who is praying and why. If we look back through chapter 4, even into chapter 3, we discover more details about the circumstances here and the people who were involved in the events leading up to this prayer. Let's come back to this in a moment!

Previously...

In Acts chapter 3, we find that Peter and John miraculously healed a lame man at the temple's Beautiful Gate. Following the miracle, Peter and John preached to the crowd of on-lookers about Jesus. They were spreading the message of the Gospel! The beginning of the next chapter describes how they were arrested and taken into custody on the charge of disturbing the people and preaching that Jesus had resurrected from the dead. They were set before a group of prominent individuals, people of power in Jerusalem. Among them were rulers, elders, scribes, Annas the high priest, Caiaphas, John, and Alexander, as well as family members of the high priest. Peter stood up, filled with the Holy Spirit, and addressed them. He said, *"Rulers of the people and elders of Israel: If we this day are judged for a good deed done to a helpless man, by what means he has been make well, let it be known to you all, and to all the people of Israel, that by the name of Jesus Christ of Nazareth, whom you crucified, whom God raised from the dead, by Him this man stands here before you whole."*

Have you ever felt like you couldn't help but speak to someone about your faith?

Then, Peter went right on ahead and, in front of those rulers, blatantly proclaimed the message of salvation (Acts 4:12). They weren't quite sure how to respond to that! They discussed among themselves what should be done to Peter and John. It was clear that they had performed an amazing and wonderful act. There was no denying that a once lame man was now walking and praising God around the temple! They decided that in order to keep word from spreading among the people about the miracle they would severely threaten the men. They called for Peter and John and commanded them not to speak or teach any longer in the name of Jesus. The answer they gave is found in two of my favorite Bible verses: *"Whether it is right in the sight of God to listen to you more than to God, you judge. For we cannot but speak the things which we have seen and heard."* They were further threatened by the authorities before finally being released.

That's when we get to this prayer. After being let go, Peter and John joined up with their companions, other believers, and filled them in on everything that had happened. They must have told them how they had been instructed to stop preaching the Gospel and stirring up the people. Then, the Bible says they raised their voice to God with one accord and lifted up the words of the prayer found in Acts 4:24-30. Who prayed this prayer? The answer is Peter, John, and fellow Christians.

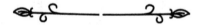

The Purpose

The purpose of the prayer can be found in Acts 4:29. They were asking God for boldness in speaking His Word by stretching out His hand to heal and so that signs and wonders might be done through the name of Jesus. They needed the courage and determination to go out and keep doing the work of the church. They wanted God to grant them the audacity to tell people about Jesus and spread the message of the Gospel even under the threat of punishment. That was why Peter and John along with their companions prayed this prayer. Knowing that they had been told to stop, they prayed that God would give them the boldness to continue and keep on telling people about Jesus.

The first-century Christians were up against devastating odds when it came to proclaiming Christ and declaring the message of the cross. They were under intense persecution that grew day by day. Sharing their faith could have resulted in imprisonment, torture, or death. There was no doubt that they needed God's help. What's so interesting about this prayer in Acts 4, is what the Christians did not request. They didn't ask for protection or safety—instead, they prayed for boldness! The word *boldness* is translated from the Greek word *parresia*, which literally means "all resolve." It carries with it the idea of confidence and having no reservations in speaking. The word also implies leaving a listener with something that deserves to be remembered or taken seriously. It's no wonder the church grew by leaps and bounds during that time!

And God Said...

God's answer can be found in the verse that immediately follows the prayer: "*And when they had prayed, the place where they were assembled together was shaken; and they were all filled with the Holy Spirit, and they spoke the word of God with boldness*" (Acts 4:31). How did God respond? He gave them boldness! The book of Acts paints a clear picture of how the church grew and grew throughout the first century. The prayer of those Christians was certainly answered with a divine "**Yes**!" They really **did** go out confidently, they really **did** speak with boldness, and they really **did** effectively spread the message of Jesus Christ.

I think it's important to stop here and remind ourselves what the Bible tells us about God's desire for mankind. Take a look at 1 Timothy 2:3-4. "*For this is good and acceptable in the sight of God our Savior, who desires all men to be saved and to come to the knowledge of the truth.*" God wants everyone to be saved. He wants everybody to come to the knowledge of the truth. That places a lot of responsibility on His children—those who have already heard, believed, and obeyed the truth. The ones who know the truth must go and share the truth, so that more people can be saved! Now, turn to 2 Peter 3:9, another verse that might be familiar to you. It says, "*The Lord is not slack concerning his promise as some count slackness; but is longsuffering toward us, not willing that any should perish, but that all should come to repentance.*" Here is another glimpse at the will of God, which is for everybody to come to repentance and for no one to perish. People can't repent if they don't know what they're turning from and what they're turning toward! They can't experience eternal life if they don't know how to obtain it! It is our duty to speak to people about Jesus, to tell them about the Gospel, to explain the importance of repentance, and to talk about what comes after this life. We cannot remain silent. We should not be content to do nothing. And if we ask for God's help in proclaiming the truth…He will give it.

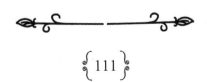

The Present

So what do we learn from all of this? What can we apply from this prayer to our own personal prayer lives? I think this prayer in Acts 4 teaches us to ask for boldness, for confidence, and for courage in speaking to people about Jesus and about the salvation that is found in Him. Is there anything of greater importance than that?

There is something even more to add to this prayer request that can be absolutely life-changing—in more ways than one! Let's consider two different Scripture references: Ephesians 6:18-20 and Colossians 4:2-4. We talked about Ephesians 6:18 in a previous chapter, and if you'll remember it immediately follows the description of the armor of God. Verses 18-20 read, "...*Praying always with all prayer and supplication in the Spirit, being watchful to this end with all perseverance and supplication for all the saints—and for me...*" (notice here that Paul is asking for his readers to continue praying for all Christians and to pray specifically for him) "...*that utterance may be given to me, that I may open my mouth boldly to make known the mystery of the gospel, for which I am an ambassador in chains; that in it I may speak boldly, as I ought to speak.*" Paul asked the Christians in Ephesus, the Christians to whom he was writing this letter, to pray for him. He even told them what to pray! He asked them to pray that the right words would be given to him, that he might speak boldly to make known the mystery of the gospel. Remember, Paul was in prison as he wrote this letter—he was actually in chains. Regardless of that fact, he asked his fellow Christians to pray for him to have the right words to speak and that he would speak them boldly. That's amazing to me.

Can you imagine what would happen if Christians across the world prayed for open doors for the Gospel?

Now, turn over to Colossians 4:2-4. Again, this is a letter from Paul written by inspiration and here he says to his readers, "*Continue earnestly in prayer, being vigilant in it with thanksgiving; meanwhile praying also for us, that God would open to us a door for the word, to speak the mystery of Christ, for which I am also in chains, that I may make it manifest, as I ought to speak.*" Paul once more asked for prayers, but this time his request was a bit different. His petition was for an "open door." He wanted prayers lifted on his behalf that he would be given an opportunity to speak about the Gospel! This letter was also written while Paul was a prisoner, and again his mind was not focused on his own current situation but on where he would take the message of Jesus next! Can you imagine what would happen if Christians across the world prayed for open doors for the Gospel?

When you put these Scripture references together, they come together in a powerful way. In one circumstance Paul asked for prayers that he might have the right words and that he would speak them boldly; in the other circumstance Paul asked for prayers that he might have the opportunity to share those words. Paul wanted doors to be opened so that he could share the Gospel, and when those opportunities presented themselves he wanted the right words to say and he wanted to say them boldly. These prayers go hand in hand!

We should follow the example of Peter, John, and the early Christians as well as Paul in praying for opportunity, utterance, and boldness when sharing the Gospel with other people. I believe with all of my heart that if we pray to God for an open door, if we ask Him for an opportunity to talk to somebody about Jesus, He **will** answer that prayer. I encourage you to make that a continual part of your prayer life. Pray for boldness when you go out into the world and talk to people about your faith. I trust that He will put somebody in your path who needs to hear the truth.

Prayer Prompt

For your prayer prompt today, I encourage you to think about Romans 1:16. This was one of the first Scriptures that came to my mind as I was thinking about something that could inspire us to pray this type of prayer. Romans 1:16 reads, "*For I am not ashamed of the gospel of Christ, for it is the power of God to salvation for everyone who believes; for the Jew first, and for the Greek.*" I don't want to be ashamed of the Gospel and I shouldn't be! The Bible says that it is the power of God to salvation. That is not something to be ashamed of at all! That's something to uphold with strength, confidence, and **boldness**. As you go into your prayer time today, beginning by saying out loud these words, "I am not ashamed of the Gospel of Christ." Then, pray for open doors, for opportunities, and for boldness as you go out and talk to people about your faith, the Bible, and about Jesus.

Don't forget that when you go out to proclaim Christ in boldness, it is also important that you also remember to speak in love. Be sure that you speak with kindness, with gentleness, and with respect. Those should all be included in our going out and talking to people about Jesus. Boldness, yes; but also right along with boldness—love, kindness, gentleness, and respect. That's so important.

I hope that this will be a blessing to you and I hope that you will consider making this a part of your daily prayer life. Let's see what will happen! Let's find out how much the church can grow! If we're praying for open doors, God will provide them. We just need to recognize those doors when they open up and be ready to step through them.

Lord, You are God, who made heaven and earth and the sea, and all that is in them, who by the mouth of Your servant David have said, 'Why did the nations rage, and the people plot vain things? The kings of the earth took their stand, and the rulers were gathered together against the Lord and against His Christ.' For truly against Your holy Servant Jesus, whom You anointed, both Herod and Pontius Pilate, with the Gentiles and the people of Israel, were gathered together to do whatever Your hand and Your purpose determined before to be done. Now, Lord, look on their threats, and grant to Your servants that with all boldness they may speak Your word, by stretching out Your hand to heal, and that signs and wonders may be done through the name of Your holy Servant Jesus.

ACTS 4:24-30

1. Who was praying in this Scripture reference and what were the circumstances leading up to this moment?

2. What was the purpose of this prayer?

3. How did God answer? What do we know about God from Scriptures like 1 Timothy 2:3-4 and 2 Peter 3:9 that explain His response to this prayer?

4. Read Ephesians 6:18-20 and Colossians 4:2-4. Who wrote these passages and what was he requesting in each of them?

5. How do these two prayer requests go hand in hand?

6. **What do we learn from these prayers that we can apply to our personal prayer lives?**

Prayer Practice

Pray for God to give you boldness in spreading the Gospel. Pray for Him to give you the words to say and an opportunity to talk to someone about Jesus. Pray that when a door opens (because it will!), you are able to recognize it and walk through it. Pray that when you share the Truth that you do it in love and kindness, with gentleness and respect. Pray for all people everywhere to come to know Jesus and the salvation that is only found in Him.

_____

_____

_____

_____

_____

_____

_____

_____

_____

Why have You afflicted Your servant? And why have I not found favor in Your sight, that You have laid the burden of all these people on me? Did I conceive all these people? Did I beget them, that You should say to me, 'Carry them in your bosom, as a guardian carries a nursing child, to the land which you swore to their fathers?' Where am I to get meat to give to all these people? For they weep all over me, saying, 'Give us meat, that we should eat.' I am not able to bear all these people alone, because the burden is too heavy for me. If You treat me like this, please kill me here and now— if I have found favor in Your sight—and do not let me see my wretchedness!

NUMBERS 11:11-15

Prayer Nine

NUMBERS 11:11-15

The Prayer

Verse 11 of Numbers 11 tells us that this was Moses talking to the Lord.

Previously...

It's clear from reading the words of this prayer that Moses was not happy with the Israelites at that particular time. What had happened among God's people that caused Moses to be so angry? If we go back to the beginning of chapter 11, we find that the Israelites were camped in the wilderness of Sinai, and they're upset because they're hungry. They're tired of the manna that God has been sending them to eat, and they want meat. They were remembering the things that they had eaten while they were in Egypt. In verse 5 it says, "*We remember the fish which we freely ate in Egypt,*

How would you describe anger that is not sinful?

the cucumbers, the melons, the leeks, the onions, and the garlic; but now our whole being is dried up; there is nothing at all except this manna before our eyes!" Remember, Moses had led them out of Egypt, out of bondage, and he was taking them on the journey that would lead them to the Promised Land. But time and time again, the Israelites complained, they did not demonstrate trust in God, and they were often punished for their unfaithfulness. In this particular situation, Moses had quite enough. He was frustrated with the people. Verse 10 says, *"Then Moses heard the people weeping throughout their families, everyone at the door of his tent; and the anger of the Lord was greatly aroused; and Moses also was displeased."* So Moses went to God in prayer.

The Purpose

The purpose of this prayer was for Moses to express his anger and frustration to the Lord over the behavior of the Israelites. What do you think about that? Do you think he was right or wrong in offering this type of prayer? Think about that for just a second and consider why you would answer one way or the other. Quite honestly, we could get into some deep discussion over this and talk about it in great detail, but for now, I'm going to suggest to you a right **and** wrong way to look at that. First, is it okay to talk to God when you're mad or upset about something? Yes. Yes, it is okay. God already knows what is making you angry. If you're feeling that emotion, or any other emotion, He already knows what you're feeling. He wants you to come and talk to Him about it. He wants you to involve Him in whatever it is that you're struggling through, whatever it is that's causing you grief or causing you pain. However, it is wrong to be disrespectful or to be irreverent in coming to God with your anger. It is wrong to put the blame on God for whatever it is that's causing you to be angry. We have to be really careful that we don't come to God in a way that accuses Him of being the instigator of our anger. We can come to God with sincere questions about things that are happening in our lives; but we shouldn't throw accusations at Him like, "Why are you doing this to me? Why have you caused this to happen? What right do you have to put this in my life?" The Bible tells us in Ephesians 4:26-27, *"Be angry, and do not sin."* Colossians 3:8 says, *"Put off anger."* And James 1:19-20 says, *"Be slow to wrath,"* or *"Be slow to anger."* The reason for these warnings is because anger can very easily cause us to trip into sin. Being angry is not sinful, but if we don't keep our anger in check and if we aren't cautious about our response to anger, it can lead us to sin.

And God Said...

There are a couple of different responses that God gave to Moses' prayer. First He said, "I'm going to give you help." Remember, in his prayer Moses cried, "I'm not able to bear all these people alone. The burden is too great for me." God heard that, and He set up a situation for Moses to have help. He instructed Moses to gather up 70 older men from among the Israelites and to bring them to the tabernacle of meeting. In verse 17, God said, "*I will take of the Spirit that is upon you and will put the same upon them; and they shall bear the burden of the people with you, that you may not bear it yourself alone.*" He gave Moses the help that he needed. Second, He provided the Israelites with meat. He sent them quail. (If you don't know that story, you'll have to go back and read it! God was displeased with the way that the Israelites were acting because of their lack of faith and their desire to return to Egypt where they believed they had it so much better. Go back and find out what happens with the quail!) God did provide. His answer to Moses' prayer was "Yes. I will give you help, and I will send food for the people."

Moses knew exactly where he needed to take his complaint. He understood that God had the answers, and he took his problem to God in prayer. Let's consider a couple of Scriptures that encourage us to do the same. In 1 Peter 5:6-7, the Bible says, "*Therefore humble yourselves under the mighty hand of God, that He may exalt you in due time, casting all your care upon Him, for He cares for you.*" When I read that verse, these words resonate in my mind: **God cares about me**. He wants me to hand my cares over to Him. The care we are to cast on Him is from the Greek word merimna, and it's an interesting word study. It literally means "to divide, or to separate from the whole." In essence, we are to give God those things that are dividing us within. Those situations, problems, people, relationships, troubles, anything that is resulting in worry, anxiety, stress, anger—emotions that cause division within our own spirits. God says, "Let Me take all of that from you, because I am concerned about you." A valuable lesson from Moses' prayer is that it is okay to bring the things that are troubling us to God and to turn them over to Him. God wants us to do that. Also, think about the words we read in Proverbs 3:5-6, "*Trust in the Lord with all your heart, and lean not on your own understanding; in all your ways acknowledge Him, and He will direct your paths.*" Moses had to trust God to help him. He had to step outside of himself, away from self-reliance, and lean on the wisdom and power of God. He had to turn to God for direction.

But wait! There is something more to learn from 1 Peter 5:6-7 and Proverbs 3:5-6 when it comes to approaching God with our problems and trusting Him for guidance that can also be related to Moses' prayer. I mentioned earlier how we need to be mindful about the way we speak to God, and the questions that Moses directs toward God are packed with blame. In my opinion, Moses should have used better judgment in the words he chose and the attitude he demonstrated in prayer. Moses asks God, "Why did You do this? Why have I not found favor with You? Did I do this; did I do that?" The Bible doesn't tell us how God felt about the way Moses spoke to Him in prayer, but we do know that it was Moses' pride that kept him out of the Promised Land. In the end, Moses elevated himself to God's level, forgetting God's sovereignty. I believe a hint of that is evident in this prayer. In 1 Peter 5:6-7, before Peter gets to the part about "casting your cares upon Him," he reminds us to humble ourselves under the mighty hand of God. In

Proverbs 3:5-6, wise Solomon tells us that in order for us to fully trust God and receive His direction, we must not lean on our own understanding. Later in Proverbs 16:18, we find the warning, *"Pride goes before destruction."* Pride is hated by wisdom (Proverbs 8:13) and with it comes disgrace (Proverbs 11:2). James writes by inspiration in his epistle that God opposes the proud and gives grace to the humble (James 4:6); and when we humble ourselves before the Lord, He will lift us up (James 4:10). Boldly approach the throne of God, tell Him everything in your heart, ask Him for the answers you're searching for, but remember that He is God, *"the King eternal, immortal, invisible, who alone is wise, and to whom honor and glory is due forever and ever"* (1 Timothy 1:17).

Know that you can talk to God in prayer about anything—even things that make you angry—but, be careful how you speak to Him. Never forget the power and the holiness of your Creator. Always remember who you're talking to when you go to Him in prayer. Keep that in mind. I love the example of Job. You know, Job had many, many things to be angry about. In Job 1:22, after everything was taken from him, the Bible says, *"In all this Job did not sin or charge God with wrongdoing."* Job is a wonderful example of someone who had many difficult and painful things happen to him but did not sin and did not place the blame on God.

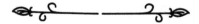

The Present

We learn from this prayer of Moses that we can go to God with our anger. God wants us to communicate with Him. He can handle the emotions we bring into His presence. But, in bringing our anger to God, we must not allow it to give rise to irreverence. God is kind, loving, and according to James 1:17, He is the giver of good gifts. God wants for us to have the things that we need on this earth and one day He wants for us to be with Him at home in Heaven. He wants that for me and for you! He does not want for us to suffer or for us to be hurt. He does not enjoy seeing His children in pain and He especially does not want for the difficult things we experience in this life to push us away from Him. The Bible tells us that God does not tempt anyone. James 1:13 says, *"Let no one say when he is tempted, 'I am tempted by God'; for God cannot be tempted by evil, nor does He himself tempt anyone."* Instead, God has said that He will always, always be there for you to help you get through the hard things, and He stands ready to share His strength with you. His loving hands are shaping the events in your life into a picture of the promise He made in Romans 8:28 that all things work together for good for those who love God and are called according to His purpose. So tell God how you feel, but do it in humility. Live according to His will in all things and trust that He will lead you in the right way.

Never forget the power and the holiness of your Creator.

Sometimes, you might find that your anger is creating a wedge between you and God and affecting your relationship with Him. It can be easy to direct our anger toward God, especially in trials that we can't explain or understand. In times like that, if you find it difficult to talk to Him in prayer, turn to someone who can help you pray. One day, I remember sitting in the car with a friend of mine who was struggling with a situation that was creating a great deal of anger in her life. She said, "I know that it's not God's fault, but I feel so angry at Him because it's happening to me." She told me that she was having a hard time finding the words to say to Him although she knew that she desperately needed His presence close to her. She asked me if I would pray with her and say the words that her heart was wrestling to say. I was happy to be able to do that for my friend, and how brave of her to reach out for help rather than slip away from God who makes all things whole.

As we wrap up our look at this prayer, I have a couple of final thoughts to leave with you. First praise God. I love that throughout the psalms we see David go to God time and time again with questions about why certain things were happening to him, but we also see that David regularly followed up his questions with praise. I think that would be a great exercise for each of us! Bring your questions with God, then praise Him for allowing you that honor. Praise Him because He cares about you. Praise Him because you need Him. Praise Him because He is in control of all things. Second, look away from yourself. Take time in situations that you are angry about to find ways to focus on other people. Shift the emphasis from yourself and what's making you mad to what you could do in your situation to help somebody else. This might not always be something you can do, but it is something to think about when you are feeling angry or frustrated.

 *Prayer Prompt*

My prayer prompt for you today begins with a look at Psalm 118:6. "The Lord is on my side; I will not fear. What can man do to me?" If you read through the rest of that psalm you'll come to this final verse: "O give thanks to the Lord, for He is good; for His mercy endures forever" (v. 29). When you're angry or frustrated and you want to talk to God about it, just remember that He is on your side. God is on your side. Don't ever forget that. Also remember that He is good. God is always good. It's His nature. He does not put things in your life to cause you misery or to make you suffer, or because He has evil intent toward you. That is not the God whom we serve. But do pray for Him to help you work through whatever it is that is causing you anger or pain. Ask for His help, His strength, His guidance, and then trust Him to stay by your side through it all.

If you have something that is on your heart that is causing you anger, something that you're working through right now that is frustrating, I encourage you to talk to God about it. Ask Him questions. Tell Him how you feel, but keep in mind who He is and who You are and be sure to approach Him in respect and humility. If you're not going through anything right now in particular that is causing you anger or frustration, just pray about situations that might be causing you anxiety. Are you worried about anything? Stressed about something? Today in your prayer time, cast your anger, your frustration, your disappointment, your stress, and your anxiety at the foot of God's throne. Give it all to Him. Give everything to Him today in prayer and ask Him to replace it all with His peace

Why have You afflicted Your servant? And why have I not found favor in Your sight, that You have laid the burden of all these people on me? Did I conceive all these people? Did I beget them, that You should say to me, 'Carry them in your bosom, as a guardian carries a nursing child, to the land which you swore to their fathers?' Where am I to get meat to give to all these people? For they weep all over me, saying, 'Give us meat, that we should eat.' I am not able to bear all these people alone, because the burden is too heavy for me. If You treat me like this, please kill me here and now--if I have found favor in Your sight--and do not let me see my wretchedness!

NUMBERS 11:11-15

1. Who was praying in this Scripture reference and what were the circumstances leading up to this moment?

2. What was the purpose of this prayer?

3. Do you think this person was right or wrong in offering this prayer? Why?

4. How did God answer this prayer?

5. Read 1 Peter 5:6-7 and Proverbs 3:5-6. How do these relate to this prayer example?

6. What do we learn from this prayer that we can apply to our personal prayer lives?

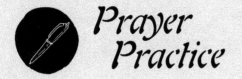

Prayer Practice

Today in your personal prayer time, talk to God about anything that has been causing you to feel angry or frustrated. Ask Him to help you put away your anger and for His help in resolving the issue, or issues, that you are facing. You can also talk to God about your worries or anything that has been making you feel anxious. Pray for Him to give you peace, clarity, strength, comfort, and guidance. Remember...He cares about you, He is on your side, and He loves you. Trust Him!

_____

_____

_____

_____

_____

_____

_____

_____

_____

_____

_____

_____

_____

_____

_____

_____

You have shown great mercy to Your servant David my father, because he walked before You in truth, in righteousness, and in uprightness of heart with You; You have continued this great kindness for him, and You have given him a son to sit on his throne, as it is this day. Now, O Lord my God, You have made Your servant king instead of my father David, but I am a little child; I do not know how to go out or come in. And Your servant is in the midst of Your people whom You have chosen, a great people, too numerous to be numbered or counted. Therefore give to Your servant an understanding heart to judge Your people, that I may discern between good and evil. For who is able to judge this great people of Yours?

1 KINGS 3:6-9

1 KINGS 3:6-9

The Prayer

King Solomon, son of God's beloved servant David, prayed these words after the Lord appeared to him in a dream and asked him to answer a life-changing question.

Previously...

At this time in Israelite history, the kingdom was being transferred from David's rule to Solomon's rule, but Solomon's transition to the throne was not exactly a smooth one. In 1 Kings 1:4, as David was nearing death, his son Adonijah declared that he would be king. Verse 4 goes on to say, *"He prepared for himself chariots and horsemen and 50 men to run before him."* Joab the commander of David's army and Abiathar the priest also followed and helped Adonijah.

When Nathan the prophet became aware of Adonijah's bold move, he spoke to Bathsheba, the mother of Solomon. He advised her to approach David and remind him about how he swore to her that Solomon would be the next king. Bathsheba did go talk to David and she revealed to him all that Adonijah had done. As she spoke to David, Nathan entered the room and confirmed everything she had said. David acted quickly. First, he assured Bathsheba that Solomon would, in fact, sit on the throne after him. Next, he gathered together Zadok the priest, Nathan the prophet, and Benaiah the valiant military leader, and instructed them to place Solomon on his mule, take him to Gihon, and anoint him king over Israel. They were to blow a horn and say out loud, "Long live King Solomon!" David went on to say, "*Then you shall come up after him, and he shall come and sit on my throne, and he shall be king in my place. For I have appointed him to be ruler over Israel and Judah*" (1 Kings 1:35).

What final words would you want to be remembered for at the end of your life?

Everything was carried out as David had directed. Solomon became king and Adonijah withdrew his attempt to take the throne. At the beginning of 1 Kings 2, David knew he was about to die, and he spoke to Solomon about some things weighing on his heart. First, he encouraged his son to be strong and to prove himself a man. Then in verse 2, David urged him with these words, "*And keep the charge of the Lord your God: to walk in His ways, to keep His statutes, His commandments, His judgments, and His testimonies, as it is written in the law of Moses, that you may prosper in all that you do and wherever you turn.*" In his last conversation with Solomon, David wanted to emphasize to Solomon the importance of following the instructions of the Lord as written in the Law of Moses. This was David's dying wish for his son: Obey God.

David died and was buried in Jerusalem after 40 years of reign over Israel. Solomon assumed the throne and soon after he ordered the deaths of Adonijah, Joab, Shimei, and the exile of Abiathar. 1 Kings 2 comes to a close with these final words, "*Thus the kingdom was established in the hand of Solomon.*" We know that Solomon loved the Lord and walked in the statutes of his father David, except that he sacrificed and burned incense in the high places (1 Kings 3:3).

Then, in 1 Kings 3:5, we read that God appeared to Solomon in a dream and said, "*Ask! What shall I give you?*"

The Purpose

God presented the new king with an open question for which there could be any answer. In other words, Solomon could have asked God for **anything**! His response to God is found in 1 Kings 3:9, "*Give to your* *servant an understanding heart to judge Your people, that I may discern between good and evil."* The prayer that Solomon brought before God in answer to His question is also recorded in 2 Chronicles 1:6-12. In verse 10, it reads, *"Now give me wisdom and knowledge, that I may go out and come in before this people; for who can judge this great people of Yours?"* Looking at both of these references, Solomon asked God for "an understanding heart" which is a heart of "knowledge and wisdom." I love the phrase "understanding heart" especially considering the original Hebrew text. The word that is translated to "understanding" is a Hebrew word that literally means "hearing." Listen to Solomon's words written this way, *"Therefore give to Your servant a hearing heart."* Isn't that a beautiful description? A hearing heart: a heart that listens attentively. In Scripture, the word *heart* refers to the mind of man, or the center of one's being. Solomon could have asked for anything, but he asked for knowledge and wisdom which originate from a mind that listens attentively.

Solomon must have remembered the final words his father David had spoken to him: *"Keep the charge of the Lord your God: to walk in His ways, to keep His statutes, His commandments, His judgments, and His testimonies, as it is written in the Law of Moses, that you may prosper in all that you do and wherever you turn"* (1 Kings 2:3). He needed wisdom to be able to discern between right and wrong and to make good choices as the ruler of a kingdom. He also knew that he had a great nation to lead and recognized his own inexperience and need for help! Solomon prayed for the wisdom to uprightly govern God's chosen people.

And God Said...

"The speech pleased the Lord that Solomon had asked this thing" (1 Kings 3:10). The Lord was pleased with the prayer of Solomon, but how did He answer? His response to Solomon is found in 1 Kings 3:11-14, *"Then God said to him: 'Because you have asked this thing, and have not asked long life for yourself, nor have asked riches for yourself, nor have asked the life of your enemies, but have asked for yourself understanding to discern justice, behold, I have done according to your words; see, I have given you a wise and understanding heart, so that there has not been anyone like you before you, nor shall any like you arise after you. And I have also given you what you have not asked for: both riches and honor, so that there shall not be anyone like you among the kings all your days. So if you walk in My ways, to keep My statutes and My commandments, as your father David walked, then I will lengthen your days."* God's answer was, "Yes! I'm going to give you what you've asked for." God gave Solomon wisdom, riches, and honor. He also told Solomon that if he would walk in His ways, or live obediently, then He would lengthen Solomon's days. This was a gift with a condition: Follow Me and I will bless you with a long life.

If you turn in your Bible to 1 Kings 4:29-34, there is another great description of God's gifts to Solomon. *"And God gave Solomon wisdom and exceedingly great understanding, and largeness of heart like the sand on the seashore. Thus Solomon's wisdom excelled the wisdom of all the men of the East and all of the wisdom of Egypt."* That description continues on through the end of the chapter, and it's clear that God abundantly answered the prayer of Solomon. In fact, God showered him with not only the things for which he **had** asked, but also for the things for which he **had not** asked. God blessed Solomon in every way!

Sadly, in the story of Solomon we discover that as his reign continued, he did not make the best choices. He allowed his heart to be led away from following after the Lord. This happened as a result of several critical choices that Solomon made and in 1 Kings 11 we are told about the most devastating of those choices. In verses 3 and 4, we learn this about Solomon: *"And he had 700 wives, princesses, and 300 concubines; and his wives turned away his heart. For it was so, when Solomon was old, that his wives turned his heart after other gods; and his heart was not loyal to the Lord his God as was the heart of his father David."* Although Solomon was granted wisdom, he still had the freedom of choice and he chose not to remain faithful. He might have been a good discerner, and maybe he judged the people well, but he didn't stay faithful and his heart followed after other gods. It seems that Solomon began to trust too much in his own wisdom rather than continue to humbly trust in God—a mistake that would affect the future of his kingdom.

As you continue to read through the life of Solomon, you find that in his later years he looked back and acknowledged the wrongs in this life. He knew that he had made bad choices and realized what was most important in life. It was an older Solomon who by inspiration authored one of the most profound statements in Scripture. At the close of the book of Ecclesiastes, the wise man Solomon summed up what is most important in life. He wrote, *"Let us hear the conclusion of the whole matter. Fear God and keep His commandments, for this is man's all. For God will bring every work into judgment, including every secret thing, whether good or evil"* (Ecclesiastes 12:13-14). This was a beautiful reflection of wisdom from a man who had lived a life marked by poor choices. In the end, Solomon said, "Listen, let me tell you what life is all about: Fear God and keep His commandments."

The Present

Where does this prayer of Solomon's fit into our lives today? Let's start by looking at James 1:5. *"If any of you lacks wisdom, let him ask of God, who gives to all liberally and without reproach, and it will be given to him. But let him ask in faith, with no doubting; for he who doubts is like a wave of the sea, driven and tossed by the wind."* Essentially, James is saying that if you need wisdom, ask God; but you can't ask and doubt that He will answer. I remember my mom telling me the story of Solomon when I was a little girl. She would say, "Lori, always pray for wisdom, because God has promised that He'll give it to you!" And so asking for wisdom has always been a regular part of my prayer life. But what exactly are we asking for when we ask for

God to give us wisdom? What is wisdom? We sometimes say that wisdom is the application of knowledge. It's taking something that we know to be true and applying it to a real-life situation. This goes right along with what we read in Proverbs 15:2, "*The tongue of the wise uses knowledge rightly, but the mouth of fools pours forth foolishness.*"

I also think of something important that Paul wrote in his second letter to Timothy. He encouraged the young man who was like a son to him, telling him that he should continue in the things he had learned and reminded him that from childhood he had known the holy Scriptures "*... which are able to make you wise for salvation through faith which is in Christ Jesus.*" Paul said that the Scriptures were **able** to make Timothy wise for salvation. From this statement, we can know this: You can study and know the Scriptures, but wisdom comes when you apply them to your life through faith. Knowing what the Bible says is one thing, but living out its teachings in your life every day is another! If you and I want to be wise when it comes to God's Word, we need to study but then we also have to let His Word shape us and change us into people who look and act like Christ.

> *You can study and know the Scriptures, but wisdom comes when you apply them to your life through faith.*

From Solomon, we learn that asking God for wisdom should be a part of our prayer lives. We can ask that God give us an understanding and a knowledge of His Word and that He will help us apply what we know in the right way. We also learn that along with praying for wisdom, we should pray for the strengthening of our faith—a faith that humbly submits to the will of God in every aspect of our lives

.

Prayer Prompt

Pray for wisdom. Make it a point today, in a special prayer, to ask for God to grant you wisdom. Proverbs 2:6 says, "For the Lord gives wisdom; from His mouth comes knowledge and understanding." If you continue reading through that chapter in Proverbs, in verses 10-12 Solomon wrote, "When wisdom enters your heart, and knowledge is pleasant to your soul, discretion will preserve you; understanding will keep you, to deliver you from the way of evil, from the man who speaks perverse things...." Wisdom will give you the ability to understand, or perceive, good and evil and to make good choices between the two. Wisdom will protect you and keep you from harm. God has said, "Ask Me for it, and if you believe I will give it to you...I will."

You have shown great mercy to Your servant David my father, because he walked before You in truth, in righteousness, and in uprightness of heart with You; You have continued this great kindness for him, and You have given him a son to sit on his throne, as it is this day. Now, O Lord my God, You have made Your servant king instead of my father David, but I am a little child; I do not know how to go out or come in. And Your servant is in the midst of Your people whom You have chosen, a great people, too numerous to be numbered or counted. Therefore give to Your servant an understanding heart to judge Your people, that I may discern between good and evil. For who is able to judge this great people of Yours?"

1 KINGS 3:6-9

1. Who was praying in this Scripture reference and what were the circumstances leading up to this moment?

2. What was the purpose of this prayer?

3. How did God feel about the prayer that was offered?

4. How did God answer the prayer?

5. Read James 1:5-6. What is promised in this verse? What is the condition?

6. **What do we learn from this prayer that we can apply to our personal prayer lives?**

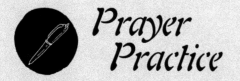

Make it a special point to ask God for wisdom in one of your prayers today. In Proverbs 2:6, we read that the Lord gives wisdom! Fully believe that He will grant your request and continue to grow in faith and knowledge of His Word so that you will make good applications of your wisdom.

_____

_____

_____

_____

_____

_____

_____

Remember now, O Lord,
I pray, how I have walked
before You in truth and with
a loyal heart, and have done
what was good in Your sight.

2 KINGS 20:3

Prayer Eleven

2 KINGS 20:3

The Prayer

Hezekiah, a king who ruled over the southern kingdom of Judah, spoke these words in a prayer to the Lord.

Previously...

Why was Hezekiah praying this prayer? Why did he want God to remember his obedience and loyal heart? First, let's talk about Hezekiah's reputation as a king. In 2 Kings 18:3-7, the Bible describes Hezekiah like this, "*And he did what was right in the sight of the Lord, according to all that his father David had done. He removed the high places and broke the sacred pillars, cut down the wooden image and broke in pieces the bronze serpent that Moses had made; for until those days, the children of Israel burned incense to it, and called it Nehushtan. He trusted in the Lord God of Israel, so that after him was none like him among all the kings of Judah, nor who were before him. For he held fast to the Lord; he did not depart from following Him, but kept His commandments, which the Lord had commanded Moses. The Lord was with him; he prospered wherever he went. And he rebelled against the king of Assyria and did not serve him."*

Hezekiah was a good king! He was a king who tried to do what was right. He obeyed God's commandments and he rid the land of the things that were used for idolatry. As a result, God was with him and Hezekiah was blessed. Continuing through the next 2 chapters, we read about the advancement of the Assyrian army, first into the northern kingdom of Israel and then into the southern kingdom of Judah. 2 Kings 18:9-11 says, *"Now it came to pass in the fourth year of King Hezekiah, which was the seventh year of Hoshea, the son of Elah, king of Israel, that Shalmaneser, king of Assyria, came up against Samaria and besieged it. And at the end of three years they took it. In the sixth year of Hezekiah, that is, the ninth year of Hoshea, king of Israel, Samaria was taken. Then the king of Assyria carried Israel away captive to Assyria."* That began Israel's time of captivity under the Assyrians. Eight years later under Sennacherib the new king of Assyria, the Assyrian army took the fortified cities of Judah. King Hezekiah even paid Sennacherib with silver from the temple and the treasuries of his own house in an effort to convince the Assyrians to withdraw from his kingdom. That wasn't enough to appease Sennacherib. He advanced his army against Jerusalem and just outside of the city he began to berate Hezekiah with insults and threats. He proclaimed that would do the same thing to Judah that he had done to other nations and take them away into captivity. At the beginning of chapter 19, the words of Sennacherib were conveyed to Hezekiah, and the king of Judah tore his clothes, covered himself with sackcloth, and went to the house of the Lord.

Hezekiah knew he needed direction from God, so he sent a message to the prophet Isaiah and asked him to pray on Judah's behalf. Isaiah's message from God to Hezekiah was this: "Don't be afraid. The Assyrians are going to retreat, and the king is going to fall by the sword in his own land." Isaiah prophesied that the kingdom of Judah would be delivered from the Assyrians; they would not be defeated by them!

In what situations have you specifically asked God for His direction?

As chapter 19 continues, we read that Sennacherib sent more warnings to Hezekiah in the form of a letter. Hezekiah spread out the letter before the Lord and prayed a beautiful prayer (vs. 15-19) asking for God to save them. Through Isaiah, God answered Hezekiah, *"Because you have prayed to Me against Sennacherib king of Assyria, I have heard."* God promised that He would defend the city of Jerusalem—that He would save it for His own sake and for the sake of His servant David. At the end of chapter 19, the Bible says that the angel of the Lord went out and killed 185,000 people in the camp of the Assyrians. The Lord fought that battle, and it was a devastating defeat for the Assyrians. Just as God foretold, Sennacherib returned home and was killed by the sword at the hands of his own sons. The kingdom of Judah was saved!

Even while the excitement of victory spread throughout the land and Hezekiah was exalted among the nations, dark days fell upon the king of Judah as a serious illness brought him near to death.

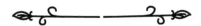

The Purpose

To understand the purpose of Hezekiah's prayer, we have to consider the context of his words. We need to look at a few verses before and after his short, one-verse prayer. 2 Kings 20:1-6 says, *"In those days Hezekiah was sick and near death. And Isaiah the prophet, the son of Amoz, went to him and said to him, thus says the Lord: 'Set your house in order, for you shall die, and not live.' Then he turned his face toward the wall, and prayed to the Lord, saying,* **'Remember now, O Lord, I pray, how I have walked before you in truth and with a loyal heart, and have done what was good in your sight.'** *And Hezekiah wept bitterly. And it happened before Isaiah had gone out into the middle court, that the word of the Lord came to him, saying, 'Return and tell Hezekiah the leader of My people, "Thus says the Lord, the God of David your father:* **I have heard your prayer, I have seen your tears; surely I will heal you.** *On the third day you shall go up to the house of the Lord. And I will add to your days fifteen years. I will deliver you and this city from the hand of the king of Assyria; and I will defend this city for my own sake, and for the sake of my servant David"''"* (emp. added).

Hezekiah was sick and his prayer was for healing. He had just been told that he was going to die, so Hezekiah reminded God how he had walked before Him in truth with a loyal heart and had done what was good in His sight. We aren't given details about how Hezekiah was feeling at the time, but we are told that he "wept bitterly," which means that he was intensely crying. With sickness within him and death at his door, Hezekiah wanted God to have mercy on him and to heal him.

And God Said...

"Yes!" God healed Hezekiah! Isaiah had not even reached the middle court of the house when the words of God came to him. God told Isaiah to go back to Hezekiah and tell him, "I've heard your prayer, I've seen your tears, and I will heal you." God said that on the third day, Hezekiah should go up to the house of the Lord, likely meaning that he should go there and give thanks to God for the healing that he'd been given. He also told Hezekiah that his life would be extended by 15 years. God's response had two parts: He healed Hezekiah **and** He extended his life.

After Isaiah told Hezekiah all that God had said, he gave the king a specific instruction. He told Hezekiah to take a lump of figs and place it on the boil. The account of Hezekiah is also found in Isaiah 38, and if we read verse 21, we're given more information about this interesting treatment: *"Now Isaiah had said, 'Let them take a lump of figs, and apply it as a poultice on the boil, and he shall recover.'"* A poultice is a paste made from herbs or plants (in this case figs) that is placed in cloth, gathered up, heated, and placed on a wound to promote healing. It's possible that the boil Hezekiah suffered with had resulted in a life-threatening infection. We're not told specifically, but we do know that the treatment of the boil resulted in Hezekiah's recovery.

However, Hezekiah told Isaiah that he wanted a sign. He heard the message from God, he complied with the fig remedy, but he wanted to know for sure that he would be healed and able to go up to the temple in three days. Isaiah told him that God would cause the shadow on the sundial of Ahaz to move backward 10 degrees, as a sign to Hezekiah that he would indeed be healed. God controlled the sun to confirm to the king that He would do what He said He would do. Hezekiah did recover and the words of praise that he wrote to God are recorded in Isaiah 38:9-20.

The Present

Does God answer our prayers for healing today? And, if He does, how does He answer those prayers? I hope that your answer to the first question is "yes," because I'm certain that you can think of many times that you've taken prayers to the throne of God for people who were sick or suffering or recovering, and have asked Him for healing. I know that those words have come out of my mouth many times in prayer. The truth is, we lift up those prayers to God quite often. When we do, I hope that we believe God can answer those prayers. If we don't believe that, why are we praying for it? So, yes, God answers prayers for healing.

Now, how does God answer our prayers for healing? One thing that we can know for sure is that God answers prayers for healing through His providence. God's providence, in this sense, refers to the special way He operates in the lives of those who do His Will, according to natural law. In other words, God works with nature or by natural means, in order to provide and care for His people. In healing, this might involve His working through people, through treatments, through medication, or through therapies in response to prayers. There are many examples in Scripture of God's use of events, people, and circumstances to accomplish something good. His providence in action! We know that God sometimes works in ways that we don't understand. Isaiah 55:8-9 reminds us that His thoughts are not our thoughts, and His ways are not our ways. Are there things that might occur in the process of healing that we don't understand or can't explain? Of course. But, when those prayers are answered, offer praise and thanks to God. In whatever way He did it, however His providence was working through those moments, trust that His hand was involved and give glory to Him for answering the prayer.

In the story of Hezekiah, we see both the miraculous work of God and the providential work of God. In healing Hezekiah, God could have instantly and completely rid him of his illness. With a snap, or a simple word, Hezekiah's boil could have disappeared and his body made whole again, but that's not the way it happened. God used Isaiah and a bunch of figs to provide the cure for Hezekiah. We don't know exactly how long it took for him to be healed, but by the third day he was ready to go to the temple. On one hand, it was a miracle that God moved the sun as a sign for Hezekiah—a demonstration of His power over the laws of nature! However, it was through natural means that He restored Hezekiah. This is a great lesson for us when we're talking about how God's providence works through prayers for healing.

Let's also consider what James 5:13-15 teaches us about prayers for healing. Those verses say, *"Is anyone among you suffering? Let him pray. Is anyone cheerful? Let him sing psalms. Is anyone among you sick? Let him call for the elders of the church, and let them pray over him, anointing him with oil in the name of the Lord. And the prayer of faith will save the sick, and the Lord will raise him up. And if he has committed sins, he will be forgiven. Confess your trespasses to one another, and pray for one another, that you may be healed. The effective, fervent prayer of a righteous man avails much."*

First, these verses teach us that we should pray for the sick and we should pray for the suffering. It says that prayers of faith will save the sick. It talks about praying for each other, so that you may be healed. This is not specifically talking about miraculous healing. It's talking about prayers of **faith**. These Scriptures are encouraging us to understand, to appreciate, and to love the power of prayer. How does prayer work? I don't always know. I'm not sure I can always give the best answer to that question. But do I believe it works? Yes. Absolutely. Do I believe God hears our prayers for healing? Yes. Without a doubt. Do I believe that it's done in and accomplished through His providence? Yes. Is that something that I can always explain? No. But I trust Him and I love him, and I know He cares for me. I know God cares for **all** the people in this world, and if it is His will, then it will be done.

> **We may not understand the way that God responds to our prayers, but we can absolutely know for certain that He loves us and that He takes care of us.**

In a small private room located just outside the entrance to the Intensive Care Unit, a woman waited as the man she loved was fighting for his life down the hall. It was in the middle of the night, and as the nursing supervisor, I had been called to come and stay with her while doctors and nurses worked to stabilize her husband. His prognosis was not good. I sat down next to her and put my arm around her. I didn't know what to say. My words seemed insufficient. The only thing I could think to do was pray with her. I asked her if that would be alright and she took my hand and said, "Yes, thank you." So I prayed. I prayed for what she wanted—healing or no more suffering. I prayed for what she needed—strength, comfort, and peace. I prayed for God's love to surround her and hold her up. I prayed for God's will to be done in all things. When the prayer ended, she hugged me tight and thanked me again. I was still with her when the doctor came in and told her that her husband had passed away. My heart ached with her as the words "We did everything we could. I'm so sorry" echoed off the walls in that small room.

I know that God heard our prayer. I know that we drew near to Him and He drew near to us. And I know that He answered our prayer—in ways that we wanted and in ways that we didn't. Prayer involves faith, surrender, and trust. It requires that we believe God is all powerful and can do anything. It demands that we hand over our fears, uncertainties, and struggles. It insists that we trust in His control, His timing, and His wisdom. We may not understand the way that God responds to our prayers, but we can absolutely know for certain that He loves us and that He takes care of us.

What specifically can we take from Hezekiah's prayer and apply to our lives? I think number one, we learn that we pray for healing, we pray for those who are sick, and we pray for those who are suffering. We pray for people who are receiving treatments and who are recovering. We lift those prayers up to God, believing that He hears us, believing that He can answer, and believing in the power of prayer. I also think we learn that we can pray for good health. The book of John 3 is a letter that was written to a man named Gaius. In verse 2 John wrote, *"Beloved, I pray that you may prosper in all things and be in health, just as your soul prospers."* John prayed for the health of his friend. This is an example of how we can pray for good health for ourselves, our families, and our friends. The prayer of Hezekiah teaches us that we can pray for those who are sick and we can pray for those who are well to remain well.

Prayer Prompt

Psalm 46:1 says, *"God is our refuge and strength, a very present help in trouble."* Remember that *refuge* can mean "shelter." God is our shelter and our strength. Let me point out the meanings of a few words: *Very* means "abundant"; *present* means the "able to find or attain"; *help* can also be translated "a helper"; and *trouble* can mean "distress" or it can also be translated to "affliction," which is something that causes pain and suffering. Look again at the second part of Psalm 46:1 with these meanings applied: "A helper who we can find abundantly when we are in distress or affliction." We won't simply find God as our helper—we will abundantly find Him—and we will abundantly find Him in times of pain or suffering, and He will be our shelter and our strength. What a beautiful and comforting thought!

Today in your prayer time, pray for something related to health. Is there somebody that you know who is suffering from something? Is there somebody that you know who is sick or in a time of recovery? I encourage you, in a special prayer today, to pray for his or her healing. If you don't know anyone who is sick right now or who could use a prayer of this nature, I encourage you to pray for good health. Pray for good health for your family, for your friends, and for yourself. Pray in faith, believing that God will answer.

Remember now, O Lord, I pray, how I have walked before You in truth and with a loyal heart, and have done what was good in Your sight.

2 KINGS 20:3

1. Who was praying in this Scripture reference and what were the circumstances leading up to this moment?

2. What was the purpose of this prayer?

3. How did God answer?

4. Does God answer this type of prayer today? In what way?

5. What is the overall lesson that James 5:13-16 is teaching about prayer?

6. What do we learn from this prayer that we can apply to our personal prayer lives?

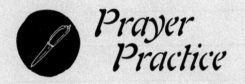

Prayer Practice

Spend time in prayer today lifting up the names of people you know who are sick, recovering from illness, or who are physically suffering in some way. Pray for healing, for comfort, and for strength. Ask God for the blessing of good health for you, your family, and your friends. Know that God is abundantly attainable as our Helper in our troubles—our distress—our pain—and our suffering (Psalm 46:1).

_____

_____

_____

_____

_____

_____

_____

_____

_____

_____

_____

_____

_____

_____

_____

_____

_____

_____

_____

_____

_____

_____

_____

_____

_____

_____

_____

_____

_____

Father, if it is Your will, take this cup away from Me; nevertheless not My will, but Yours, be done.

LUKE 22:42

Prayer Twelve

LUKE 22:42

The Prayer

This prayer was prayed by our Lord and Savior Jesus Christ just before His betrayal by Judas, His arrest, His trial, and ultimately, His crucifixion on the cross. While in the Garden of Gethsemane, He spent time in prayer with His Father before the final agonizing hours of His life.

Previously...

Jesus lived thirty-three years on this earth knowing that His journey here would ultimately lead Him to the cross. Even before God the Father spoke His creation into existence, God the Son knew He would have to give His life as a sacrifice in order for mankind to be saved. Knowing that, He still prayed in anguish for there to be another way as His suffering and death drew closer. But there was no other way to make atonement for the sin that separated man from God. It required the blood of a perfect Lamb: our Savior, Jesus Christ.

The first prophetic message of hope for mankind is declared just three chapters into the book of Genesis; and the last one echoes from the final verses of Revelation. From beginning to end, the Bible tells the story of a Redeemer who came into the world to defeat Satan, to save people from sin and death, to offer hope for eternal life, and who is coming back one day to take His family Home. That Redeemer is Jesus. Let me tell you about Him...

God is three personalities in one: God the Father, God the Son, and God the Holy Spirit. Jesus is God the Son.

He is divine and eternal.

He accomplished God's eternal purpose through His death and establishment of the church.

After creation, over a period of 4000 years, His coming as the Messiah—Redeemer and Deliverer—was prophesied and anticipated.

When the time had come according to God's plan, Jesus was conceived by the power of the Holy Spirit and born to a virgin named Mary.

He was born in a stable, wrapped in blankets, and slept in a manager.

He learned the trade of carpentry from His earthly father Joseph.

He had brothers and sisters.

He grew and developed in all the ways people do—physically, spiritually, mentally, and socially.

He understood His purpose to do the will of God as a young boy and He lived in obedience to God's will His entire life.

At about age 30, He began His ministry as a teacher and revealed Himself as the prophesied Messiah.

He chose 12 men—mostly fishermen, along with a tax collector, a thief, and a zealot—to be His closest friends, confidantes, and co-workers.

He drew large crowds—of men, women, and children—and they followed Him wherever He went.

He performed miracles—healed the sick, restored vision to the blind, cast out demons, demonstrated power over space, time, and matter, and raised the dead.

He felt compassion for people and met their needs—physically and spiritually.

He prayed to God often.

He loved people...all people...including the rejected, the hated, and the oppressed.

He listened and asked people questions.

He talked to people about the kingdom of Heaven.

His teachings emphasized love, kindness, forgiveness, obedience, trust, faith, humility, and service to others.

He was concerned with the hearts of people.

He felt every emotion and was tempted in every way.

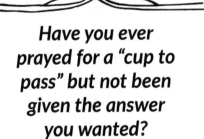

Have you ever prayed for a "cup to pass" but not been given the answer you wanted?

He never sinned. Not once. Even though the devil must have worked hard to make Him fall—knowing that just **one** sin, just one, would be enough to destroy God's plan to save man.

He lived His life in the shadow of the cross, knowing the pain and shame it would bring but choosing to never quit...to submit to the will of His Father even to His very last breath—because of the joy and hope He wanted to give to people.

The Purpose

Jesus asked His Father in prayer to take "this cup" away from Him. What did Jesus mean? What "cup" did He want to have removed? The phrase that He used—"this cup"—was a common expression of the time. It referred to an experience, or a divine appointment, that was either good or bad. It could be joyful or not. The Greek Lexicon says it was something either favorable or unfavorable. Jesus faced a painful experience that He knew He would have to endure. In His case, "this cup" referred to suffering. The cup from which Jesus would have to drink was going to be agony and it was going to be death. Jesus prayed for the cup of suffering to be taken away from Him. Jesus prayed, "Is there any other way, Father, to accomplish your plan of salvation?" In Matthew's account of this same event, Jesus asked three times for God to take the cup away, to let it pass. In that humble request, we see the human side of Jesus not wanting to endure the brutal humiliation, the severe pain, and the horrific death on the cross. Then, with a strength and a love that we cannot comprehend, Jesus said to His Father, "Not what I want, God, but let what You want—what is according to Your plan—let **that** be done. Not My will, but Yours."

And God Said...

God's answer was, "No. I can't take this cup away from You. There is no other way. This is how My eternal purpose is going to be accomplished. This is how salvation is going to be offered to mankind. It will take a perfect sacrifice to make atonement for the sins of the world, one time for all time. You are the only way." And Jesus drank from that cup. He went through the suffering. He was tortured and crucified on the cross so that mankind could have redemption and salvation. He didn't want to go through it, but He prayed for God's will to be done.

The Present

This prayer of Jesus is an extraordinary example of what our attitude should be as children of God. 1 John 5:14 says, "*Now this is the confidence that we have in Him, that if we ask anything according to His will, He hears us.*" We can have no doubt that God hears us when we ask for anything according to His will. Our attitude in prayer should be, "It's not what I want, Father, it's what You want. Let Your will be done in my life—accomplish Your desire, Your purpose for me. Help me to live according to Your word, Your ways, Your commands." That's what it means to pray for God's will. It's wanting what He wants to be accomplished in your life. When you pray for that, you have the assurance that He hears you, and ultimately God will be glorified. Of all the prayers we've studied, all of the different purposes served in prayer, and all of the reasons to pray, perhaps this prayer of Jesus is the most important and all-encompassing: to ask for God's will to be done in your life. Our prayer should always be "Not my will, God, but Yours be done."

Our prayer should always be, "Not my will, God, but Yours be done."

Jesus was crucified on a cross and buried but did not remain in the grave. He rose again. He defeated death and with that final act of divine, powerful love He secured our hope for eternal life in Heaven. He is there now. Preparing a place for His people. Sitting on the right hand of God. Speaking words of mercy and grace in our defense to the Father, because He understands what it's like to live on this earth.

I like to imagine Jesus sitting here next to me at the table where I write. I actually think about it often. I look at the chair where I picture Him sitting and I even talk to Him, not in prayer, but like He's a friend sharing a cup of coffee with me. He listens to me talk about what I'm struggling with, He smiles and laughs with me when I talk to Him about my children, He reassures me and tells me it's okay when I apologize for the many ways I fall short of who I should be. I cherish our "conversations" because I never leave feeling inadequate or harshly judged—I always leave feeling encouraged, uplifted, strengthened, and loved. He makes me want to be better, but at the same time always makes me feel like I'm just enough.

I hope you know Jesus. I haven't even told you a fraction of His story—there's so much more to say! Jesus is your lifesaver and life-changer. He is your Redeemer. He is your Friend. He gave up everything for you and He would do it again. If you don't know Him, just stop...be still...and listen...because He is standing at the door of your heart and knocking. He loves you and wants so much for you to let Him in.

Prayer Prompt

Today pray for God's will to be done in your life and through your life. Trust that He will guide you and that He will take care of you. When you live a life that is characterized by trust in God, there are amazing things that happen. First, you will be able to let go of burdens that weigh heavy in your heart and give them to God. Worry, stress, frustration, anger, resentment—all of those feelings and emotions that make your spiritual walk more difficult—are dropped at the foot of God's throne when you trust His plan for your life. And, His plans are always perfect because **He** is perfect! When you live a life of trust, you will be driven to live a life of obedience. The two go hand in hand. If you trust God, then you believe what He has said and you do what He has commanded, knowing that He loves you and wants the best for you. You are His child! In trusting God, you also remember all of the extraordinary promises He has made—those He has already kept and those He is keeping even now. *"I won't leave you, I'll forgive you, I'll make you a way out of temptation, I'll work all things together for your good..."* and the list goes on and on and on. God has always provided for His people. We see it time and again on the pages of our Bibles and He is still doing it today.

Pray that God will help you let go of your will and replace it with His. Pray that He will give you a spirit of understanding and a spirit of strength so that whatever cup you are given to drink, if it is His will, you will drink

.

Father, if it is Your will, take this cup away from Me; nevertheless not My will, but Yours, be done.

LUKE 22:42

1. Who was praying in Luke 22:41-42 and what was happening at this particular moment?

2. What was the purpose of this prayer?

3. How did God answer, and why?

4. What did God accomplish through Jesus Christ? (Ephesians 2:14-16, 19-22; 3:8-13)

5. According to Hebrews 12:2, why did Jesus endure the cross? What does that mean?

6. Read 1 John 5:14. What does this Scripture tell us about the confidence we should have in God?

7. What do we learn from this prayer that we can apply to our personal prayer lives"

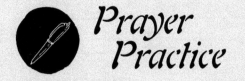

Prayer Practice

Today pray for God's will to be done in your life and through your life. Pray that He will help you and direct your life as you commit to trusting Him and obeying Him. Ask that God will help you let go of your will and replace it with His. Pray that He will give you a spirit of understanding and a spirit of strength so that whatever cup you are given to drink, if it is His will, you will drink.

_____

_____

_____

_____

_____

_____

_____

_____

_____

_____

_____

_____

_____

_____

_____

_____

_____

_____

Learning to Love Prayer

AND now, we've nearly come to the end! We began with a look at the privilege and practice of prayer, then closely examined a collection of prayers from the Bible, each one teaching us a unique purpose for prayer. As we bring this study to a close, let's review the prayers we've discussed and organize them into a table that can serve as a helpful reference for you in the future.

Putting it all together...

At the end of this chapter, there is a blank table that you can use to fill in the purpose of each of the twelve prayers we've studied in this book. Beginning with #1, we looked at the prayer of Hannah. Hers was a prayer offered in a time of waiting. Next, we talked about Samson. Samson's prayer was for strength in a specific moment. It was a prayer for STAN: Strength To Act Now! Then, we looked at one of the prayers of David. It was a prayer of gratitude and thanksgiving. Our fourth prayer was one of Daniel's. His prayer was one of confession. He confessed the sins of Israel and asked God for forgiveness. After that was Paul's prayer in Ephesians chapter 3, and it was a prayer that was specifically for other people. He prayed for the good of others, specifically for Christians. Mary's prayer came next, and hers was a prayer of praise. She lifted up praise to God for being the one chosen to carry Jesus Christ the Messiah. Prayer #7 was the prayer of Jehoshaphat. He prayed for help and guidance when he didn't know what to do. Next was the prayer of Peter and John and some of their fellow Christians. They prayed for boldness in telling people about Jesus and spreading the Gospel. Following that was the prayer of Moses. His prayer was for expressing anger. He took his feelings of frustration to God in prayer. Prayer #10 belonged to Solomon. He prayed for wisdom, an understanding heart, and for the ability to discern between good and evil. Then came the prayer of Hezekiah. He prayed for healing. The last prayer was spoken by Jesus, and He prayed for God's will to be done in and through His life.

Stop for just a moment and look again at all of those unique and meaningful prayer focuses. I encourage you to review that table from time to time and incorporate those types of prayers into your own prayer life. There are many more prayers that we could look at in the Bible, and you can even continue this study on your own. Find a Bible prayer and ask yourself: Who was praying, why were they praying, and how did God answer the prayer. Each one will deepen your love and appreciation for the tremendous spiritual blessing we have in prayer.

Embracing the Blessing...

Knowing the whys and hows of prayer is the right place to start, but how do we embrace it as a part of our everyday lives? How do we learn to love prayer? I'm going to give you some suggestions that might help. These might sound simple, but they are profoundly important and can change your prayer life significantly. Here are four things to consider as you pursue a heart of prayer:

1. **To learn to love to pray, you have to pray.** The best way to have a better prayer life is to start praying. Choose it! Decide to make it a priority. Come up with a prayer plan and establish a routine. What you'll find is that once you begin praying consistently, you'll miss it when it's not a part of your day. Begin with a small goal. For example, commit to pray every day for one week. At the end of a week, come up with a new goal that will challenge you a little more. Once you create a daily prayer habit, work on praying more throughout each day.

   You and I will never be perfect when it comes to prayer. We may not have just the right words, we may not have just the right focus, and we may not even ask for just the right things, but we have to let all of that go and just start to pray. The truth is, we'll only become stronger in those areas if we stop expecting perfection and begin having real and regular conversations with God.

2. **Don't settle for easy.** In the process of growing and developing your prayer life, you have to know that it won't always be easy. You'll have to work at it, but it is so worth the time and effort. The benefits far outweigh the challenges. There's a story that's found in 1 Kings 12 that I want to talk about here, because it's a good reminder that we should never be satisfied with the easy road. To give you a little background, at the end of chapter 11, Solomon has died. Following his death, the Israelite nation split into two separate kingdoms: the kingdom of Israel in the north and the kingdom of Judah in the south. Judah was being ruled by Solomon's son, Rehoboam, and Israel was being ruled by a man named Jeroboam. Jeroboam was not a good king. He made some really bad choices. He

didn't want to lose the people of his kingdom to Rehoboam. He was afraid that they would turn back to Rehoboam and pledge their loyalty to him. Jeroboam wanted to keep them under his reign and in his kingdom, and so he did some things to help make that happen. One of his plans involved keeping the people of his kingdom from traveling down to the city of Jerusalem (located in the southern kingdom of Judah) to worship in the temple. Verse 26 of 1 Kings 12 says, *"And Jeroboam said in his heart, Now the kingdom may return to the house of David. If these people go up to offer sacrifices in the house of the Lord at Jerusalem, then the heart of this people will turn back to their lord, Rehoboam king of Judah, and they will kill me and go back to Rehoboam king of Judah. Therefore the king asked advice, made two calves of gold, and said to the people, 'It is too much for you to go up to Jerusalem. Here are your gods, O Israel, which brought you up from the land of Egypt!' And he set one in Bethel, and the other he put in Dan. Now this thing became a sin, for the people wept to worship before the one as far as Dan."* Verses 31 through 33 describe how Jeroboam made priests from men who were not of the tribe of Levi and ordained feasts that had not been instituted by God. He was turning the people away from following after the commandments of God and turning them toward idolatry. Look again closely at the words of Jeroboam in verse 28. He told the people of his kingdom, "It is too much for you to go to Jerusalem. That's too hard. It's too far." Then he made two golden calves, and said, "Here are your gods that brought you out of Egypt! These are the gods for you to worship!" He set up one in Bethel and put the other one in Dan. He turned his people away from going to worship in the house of God by giving them something that was easier, something to settle for. Don't let that happen to you. Choose the journey that is going to take you to God's dwelling place. Don't be satisfied with the calf in Bethel and the calf in Dan. Don't settle for that. When you go to God in prayer, you are approaching Him at His throne. You are bringing yourself into the presence of God. Don't be content with anything less. Don't settle for easy.

> **Choose the journey that is going to take you to God's dwelling place**

3. **Take God's presence with you everywhere.** One of the things that I say over and over to my children, is that when you face a situation, any situation, it could be one that is stressful, one that is worrisome, one that is painful, one that is tempting or trying or scary, the first thing that you want to do is to invite God into that situation, whatever it is! Welcome Him in. Involve Him in everything that you do—in every decision that you have to make, in every problem that you encounter, in every illness or struggle that you might experience. Bring in God, first. Take His presence with you everywhere. I think of Moses in Exodus 33. In verse 1, God had just told Moses that it was time for them to leave Sinai and continue their journey to the promised land. Moses declared to Him in verse 12, *"You say to me, 'Bring up this people,' but You have not let me know whom You will send with*

me. Yet, You have said, 'I know you by name, and you have also found grace in My sight.'" He wanted to know who God was going to send with him on that journey. God answered and said in verse 14, *"My presence will go with you, and I will give you rest."* Moses responded by saying, *"If Your presence will not go with me, do not bring us up from here"* (v.15). Moses says if You're not going with us, don't bring us up from here. He wanted the assurance that God would be with them. In the same way, you want God's presence to go with you everywhere. Don't go anywhere without Him and invite Him into everything through prayer.

4. **Think about the day you will meet God face to face.** ***Will you already be friends?*** I think about this often. I think about that day that I go Home, and I meet God. Will it be like seeing an old friend? Will He know me because I have talked to Him through all these years? Will it be like a loving reunion? You don't want that day to come and have it be an awkward, "Well, I know who You are, but we haven't really talked" moment. You want it to be like you are two friends who are finally getting to meet face-to-face. I love the song "My God and I" because of its lovely description of being together with God. *"My God and I go in the field together, we walk and talk as good friends should and do; we clasp our hands, our voices ring with laughter, my God and I walk through the meadow's hue."* What a beautiful picture of you and God as friends. Start that relationship now. Nurture it and allow it to grow. Develop that special connection between you and God through prayer. There's not one other person that you need by your side as you go through this life. Talk to Him every day, throughout the day, about everything. Listen to Him by reading and studying His Word. Spend time with Him—your Creator, your Father, and your Friend.

Spend time with Him... your Creator, your Father, and your Friend.

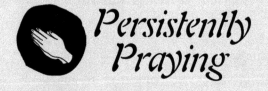

Persistently Praying

And that leaves me with your ongoing prayer prompt, the one that is just going to carry on from day to day. Remember 1 Thessalonians 5:17: *"Pray without ceasing."* Have a special time in prayer: a private, intimate, conversation time where you talk to God in secret, in your own place, where you can have no distractions. Have that time. But then also, pray continually. Pray throughout the day. When a time comes for you to give praise, or to offer a confession, or to pray on behalf of someone else, or to pray for strength, take hold of those opportunities and pray. Make that just a part of who you are and what you do in any given moment.

That brings me to the end, and I leave this study in your hands. I pray that it has been a blessing to you and that your prayer life will be strengthened. I'm thankful for the Scriptures that were written for our learning (Romans 15:4) and I'm happy for the privilege to share with you these prayers of the Bible that help us realize even more the hope that is found in Christ. It's only because of Him that we can come before God with our spoken words of praise, confession, gratitude, and need. It's only because of Him that we will one day be at Home with our Father in Heaven. While we wait, we look forward to that day, and share our lives with Him through prayer. Peace and love to you always. LB

Putting It All Together...

THE PERSON	A PRAYER FOR:	THE PERSON	A PRAYER FOR:
1. Hannah		7. Jehoshephat	
2. Samson		8. Peter, John, and fellow Christians	
3. David		9. Moses	

THE PERSON	A PRAYER FOR:	THE PERSON	A PRAYER FOR:
4. Daniel		10. Solomon	
5. Paul		11. Hezekiah	
6. Mary		12. Jesus	

Embracing the Blessing...

1. To learn to love to pray, you have to _____!

2. Don't settle for _____! (Choose the journey that will take you to God's dwelling place; don't be satisfied with idols in Dan or Bethel! [1 Kings 12:27-30]).

3. Take God's _____ with you everywhere! (Exodus 33:15).

4. Think about the day you'll meet God face to face...will you already be

_____?

Prayer Practice

"Pray without ceasing" (1 Thessalonians 5:17). As this study has come to an end, take the opportunity here to write down specific goals that will help keep you in conversation with God. Refer back to the first couple of chapters and reflect again on your obstacles and what you can do to remove them or move around them. Then, review the practical tips and decide which ones you can implement in your everyday life. Most importantly, ask for God's strength and guidance as you continually pursue a heart of prayer.

_____

_____

_____

_____

_____

_____

_____

_____

_____

_____

_____

CPSIA information can be obtained
at www.ICGtesting.com
Printed in the USA
LVHW021845160723
752622LV00053B/1327

9 781952 955044